Out of the Shadows

Penny,

Blessings,

Carolyn A. Roth

Dr. Carolyn A. Roth

Out of the Shadows

Exposing the Power of Bible Women

Out of the Shadows, Exposing the Power of Bible Women

Unless otherwise identified in the narrative, Scripture quotations, Chronological Tables, Maps and Introductions to individual books of the Bible, are taken from the *Archeological Study Bible* (2005) a derivative of *Holy Bible New International Version Study Bible.*® NIV®. Copyright ©1973, 1978, 1984 by International Bible Society. Used by Permission of Zondervan. All rights reserved.

Scripture quotations marked (AMP) are taken from the *Amplified Bible*, copyright ©1954, 1958, 1962, 1964, 1965, 1987 by The Lockman Foundation. Used by permission.

Scripture quotations marked (ESV) are from the *Holy Bible, English Standard Version Study Bible* ® copyright © 2001, 2008 by Crossway Bibles, a publishing ministry of Good News Publishers. Used by permission. All rights reserved.

Cover: Create Space

Publisher Imprint: Carolyn Roth Ministry (www.CarolynRothMinistry.com).

ISBN: 978-1946919007, Soft cover

Contents

Preface..5

Section 1: Identifying Power and Influence.......................7

    Chapter 1 Personal Power.....................................9
    Chapter 2 Positional Power.................................23
    Chapter 3 Will Power..38
    Chapter 4 Influence, Power in Action.....................44

Section 2: 10 Bible Women Who Used Power....................61

    Chapter 5 Eve, Not Second Best...........................62
    Chapter 6 Sarah, Relationship Power in Action............70
    Chapter 7 Moses's Mothers and Wives....................80
    Chapter 8 Deborah, Tower of Influence....................89
    Chapter 9 Samson, Surrounded by Women................98
    Chapter 10 Bathsheba, Making the Best of It.............107
    Chapter 11 Jezebel, Consistent Influencer................116
    Chapter 12 Esther, From Influenced to Influencer........125
    Chapter 13 Mary, Doubtful Influencer....................134
    Chapter 14 Jezebel of Thyatira, Negative Power.........141

Conclusions..148

References Cited..150

Dr. Carolyn A. Roth Bio...152

Preface

God created both a woman and a man. Despite sermons and seminars to the contrary, God created women to be no less powerful than men. Most Bible women weren't in formal power-positions, yet, they were powerful. Women didn't wield power through military might, politics, or economic achievements. They exercised power in more subtle ways. The primary way women plied their power was through positive influence, i.e., rational, social, and emotional. At times, Bible women used negative influence techniques to get their way; they weren't opposed to using manipulation, intimidation, and threats.

Like me, you probably noticed that the Bible was written by men. Often, these men gave little information on women. I've come to suspect that the lack of information about Bible women was because male scripture writers had little insight into what women felt or thought. Their lack of understanding of women often made it hard for them to interpret women's behavior. Perhaps, male Bible writers couldn't recognize either a woman's power or her influence.

Out of the Shadows is a book about the power and influence of Bible women. In order to evaluate how Bible women were powerful and influential, power and influence require working definitions. I chose to use definitions of management researcher, Dr. Terry Bacon. Section 1, Identifying Power and Influence, gives definitions and descriptions of types of power and influence. Included are examples, usually from both the Old Testament and New Testament, where a woman used that type of power or influence. Section 2 (chapters 5-14) contains individual stories of powerful and influential Bible women. Each woman had several power sources and used a variety of influence strategies to achieve their goals in a world where they were anything but victims.

Out of the Shadows is much more than just another book that lists women in the Bible. The focus is the power of Bible women exhibited through their influence. I explore, and at times give my explanations about, what a Bible woman could have been thinking when she consciously or unconsciously influenced the ideas and behaviors of individuals in her world. Bible women were not all "good" women. At times they were more interested in getting their way than in being admired.

The book was written, not for clergy nor for academicians, but for Christian laypersons like you and me. Women will nod their heads when they read some of these women's behaviors, even when behaviors were less than beneficial. After all, Bible women's emotions, motives, and behaviors were reality. When men read these stories, they may identify with male Bible characters. They remember times when their minds and behaviors were changed by words or actions of a woman. For both genders, the book stimulates self-awareness.

Increasingly, individuals from different faiths, i.e., Muslim, Hindu, and atheists turn to the Bible for insight into the Christian belief system. They want to understand Christian women's behavior. Often non-Christian women who read the Bible without interpretation ask themselves, "Why would I want to be a Christian woman? Does the Christian God value women? Weren't Bible women a bunch of chattels?" These seeking women can use *Out of the Shadows* as an adjunct to the Bible as they come to realize that God never meant women to be second best. The book is a much-needed compilation of Bible women's actions.

Identifying Bible Women's Behaviors

Individuals use power to get something they want, that is, to get things done. Sway and clout are synonyms of power. When an individual has power over another, he/she can influence the other person's behavior. Both men and women use the same types of power. Most Bible women's power sources were the same as those of 21st century women. They used five personal power sources and five positional power sources.[1] Personal power sources were knowledge, expressiveness often call eloquence, attraction, character, and relationship (history). The primary positions of Bible women were: member of a family, clan, tribe, nation, and in some instances a guild. Positional power sources were role, resources, information, network, and reputation.

Each power source can become a power drain or take away from a woman's power. A simple example is embodied in knowledge power. When a woman's knowledge was correct and timely, she became more powerful; but, what if a woman gave wrong or outdated information? Then, she lost knowledge credibility. She could no longer influence others using her knowledge power. Others stopped acting on what she said.

Some Bible women had tremendous will power. Will is more than a desire for power. Will power requires a user to act on her desire for power. Management guru Terry Bacon called will power a "mega-source of power" because it magnified every other power source.[1] Will power requires passion, commitment, energy, and action. Often Bible women with will power defied obstacles, overcame failures, and moved out of traditional women's roles. They worked hard to acquire knowledge, build connections, and amass resources and information.

Power is neither moral nor immoral. Mostly Bible women used their power to benefit others; but, sometimes they used it to harm others. Occasionally, their power actions got just the opposite effect from what they intended. An example occurred early in the Bible in Genesis. Eve wanted knowledge for herself and Adam. In her mind knowledge was good. Fruit from a special tree would give her and Adam knowledge. Eve used both her role as Adam's wife and attractiveness to encourage Adam to eat fruit from the forbidden Tree of Knowledge of Good and Evil (Genesis chapter 3). Eve didn't conceive that eating forbidden fruit would get the two of them expelled from their garden home.

Two verses in the Bible summarize God's perspective on power. The first is that power belongs to God (Psalm 62:11). Nothing on earth occurs, be it a cataclysmic event, a queen crowned, or a flower dropping a petal, unless God wills the event. God is sovereign over all the earth and all that happens on it, under it, and above it. The second Bible verse about power instructs powerful individuals how to act: "Do not withhold good from those to whom it is due, when it is in your power to act" (Proverbs 3:27).

A woman's influence came from her power. Without power, women had no influence. Let me write that again just so readers know the relationship between power and influence: without power, women had no influence! Influence can be both positive and negative.[1] Positive influence strategies are rational, social, and emotional. Negative influence tactics are avoidance, intimidation, manipulation, and threat. In the Bible women used a myriad of influence techniques, some were positive and some were negative.

To set the stage to study Bible women's power and influence, I reviewed two categories of power, personal and positional (organizational), as well as will power. Read about power sources in chapters 1-3. Chapter 4 contains the influence techniques that Bible women used. You may be tempted to skip the remainder of Section 1, thinking "how dry." Don't do it! This material sets the stage for understanding and interpreting Bible woman's power and influence. Further, for each type of power and influence, I give at least one example of where Bible women used it. If you ever wondered about the strength of Bible women, read these chapters.

Chapter 1

Personal Power

Bible women had goals and objectives separate from those of fathers, husbands, brothers, and other men in their environments. Intuitively, they understood that if they wanted to make a difference in their environment—whether that environment was a home, harem, tribe, or kingdom—they had to be powerful. Woman wanted a variety of things. Mary and Martha wanted Jesus to bring their dead brother back to life. Jochebed wanted to keep her new-born son (Moses) alive. Herodias wanted the head of John the Baptist. These women and other Bible women used their personal power to get what they wanted. Personal power includes knowledge, eloquence (expressiveness), attraction, character, and relationships (history). In both the Old and New Testament, women understood that power to influence individuals, especially men, began with themselves.

Knowledge Power

How many times did you hear, "knowledge is power" as your mother pried you out of bed in the morning for school? She didn't just conjure this saying; it's from the Bible. Proverbs 24:5 reads, "A wise man is …. better than a strong man, and a man of knowledge increases and strengthens his power" (AMP). Perhaps more importantly in a book on Bible women, an ideal woman is one who "opens her mouth in skillful and godly wisdom" (Proverbs 31:26 AMP). In every culture, Israelite, Egyptian, Persian, Roman, etc., where Bible women lived, knowledge was a powerful resource. Bible writers recognized that some women had knowledge power while other women didn't. The Bible is replete with stories about knowledgeable women.

Knowledge isn't just what a person knows, that is, their learning and wisdom. Knowledge encompasses skills, abilities, talents, and accomplishments. Today, often we figure out an individual's knowledge by looking at their credentials: PhD, EdD, JD; their title or position: doctor, professor, senator, prime minister; and their affiliations and honors: Mensa, Oxford, MIT, Nobel Prize, or Olympic Medal. Bible women had none of these designations. Most of them couldn't read or write; yet their actions proved that they had knowledge and ability, and ultimately power.

Knowledge gives power only when others recognize and value it.[1] When a Bible woman had knowledge, but no one knew about her knowledge or her knowledge was irrelevant to the situation, then her knowledge didn't increase her power base. Timing is important in knowledge power. Consider a woman who had a piece of knowledge, which she shared at just the moment when the knowledge was needed. Individuals talked about her contribution. She was seen as a power source. Hearers looked up to her.

One of the best examples of knowledge power in the Old Testament was the queen mother in Babylon. The setting for this Bible story was a banquet given by King Belshazzar, son of King Nebuchadnezzar (Daniel chapter 5). At the banquet Belshazzar ordered gold and silver vessels from the Jerusalem temple brought to the banquet hall so he, his lords, and wives could drink from them. As the nobles praised the gods of gold and silver, a finger of a man's hand wrote on a wall in the banquet hall. King Belshazzar was terrified, his color changed, his knees actually knocked together. None of the astrologers, magicians, and diviners could interpret the words on the wall. Finally, the queen mother entered the banquet hall. She told King Belshazzar that Daniel, a man brought to Babylon from Judah by her husband King Nebuchadnezzar, could interpret the writing on the wall. Daniel was brought to the banquet hall. He told Belshazzar what the words said and meant to the Babylonian kingdom.

The Bible didn't record the name of Nebuchadnezzar's queen and the mother of Belshazzar; however, she had power. Her power was knowledge of Daniel and his skills, knowledge unknown to Belshazzar's nobles and wise men. We have no idea what happened to this royal woman; but, in this time and place hers was the most powerful voice in the room. Notice the timing of the queen mother's input. She waited to enter the king's banquet hall until after all of the magicians and supposed wise men admitted that they couldn't interpret the writing on Belshazzar's banquet wall. The queen mother willingly shared her knowledge to benefit the king.

In the New Testament, Priscilla had knowledge power. When Emperor Claudius exiled Jews from Rome, Priscilla and her husband, Aquila, went to Corinth. In Corinth they met Paul and started a Christian church in their home. Later, the couple traveled to Ephesus with Paul and again started a home church. Bible historians identified both Priscilla and Aquila as deacons in the early Church. Luke and Paul sometimes referred to the couple as Priscilla and Aquila and at other times as Aquila and Priscilla. Apparently, Priscilla had equal status with her husband in churches they started.

One Sabbath Priscilla and Aquila heard a visitor, Apollos, speaking in the Ephesus synagogue (Acts 18:24-26). Apollos was a learned Jewish scholar from Alexandria, Egypt. Apollos spoke eloquently about the coming of Messiah, but, he knew only the baptism of repentance preached by John the Baptist. After the synagogue meeting, Priscilla and Aquila invited Apollos to their home. There, they explained the life and death of Jesus and that Jesus was the expected Messiah. Through Priscilla and Aquila sharing their knowledge of Jesus, a strong missionary voice was added to the new Christian church.

Expressive Power

Expressiveness, sometimes called eloquence, is a person's ability to communicate powerfully and effectively.[1] Eloquent individuals were viewed as more effective leaders than those who weren't eloquent. Most Bible women expressed themselves through words. Ruth was a Bible woman with expressive power. Here is Ruth's story:

Naomi, an Israelite woman along with her husband and two sons, relocated to Moab because of a famine in the Bethlehem region. While in Moab, Naomi's husband died. Both of Naomi's sons married Moabite women, Orpah and Ruth. Then, both sons died. Determined to return to Bethlehem, Naomi directed her daughters-in-law to return to their Moabite families. Orpah went; however, Ruth refused to leave Naomi. Ruth's words to Naomi were: "Don't urge me to leave you or to turn back from you. Where you go I will go, and where you stay I will stay. Your people will be my people and your God my God. Where you die I will die, and there I will be buried. May the Lord deal with me, be it ever so severely, if even death separates you and me" (Ruth 1:16-17).

Powerful expression has three requirements: it is substantive, concise, and correct.[1] Substantive means that the words move the line of thought forward and are relevant to the topic. Ruth's words were relevant and essentially ended the conversation between herself and Naomi. Ruth wasn't about to leave Naomi despite Naomi's encouragement for her to go back to her family. Ruth was concise in her response to Naomi. She included no empty words, no fillers, no verbal pauses. Finally, Ruth's assertion was grammatically correct (or whoever recorded Ruth's words made them grammatically correct). When we read this passage, word selection, sentence structure, and grammar seem ideal.

The human brain loves patterns and repetitions. When speakers used word patterns and repetitions, what they said was remembered. Ruth's words to Naomi have been memorized and often repeated in wedding vows. They resonated with each of us who have loved another person and wanted to be with that person. I believe these 66 words were a reason the book of Ruth was included in the Canon of Scripture.

Effective speakers fill their speeches with images and metaphors that create pictures in listener's minds. In the New Testament, Jesus went to the Gentile area of Tyre and Sidon. He stayed in a private home. Jesus wanted to rest. He didn't want anyone to know he was there; but, a local woman learned that Jesus was in the town. She went to the home where he stayed. She begged him to heal her daughter (Mark 7:24-30). The daughter was possessed by a demon. Initially, Jesus refused to heal the daughter, saying that it wasn't right to take children's bread and toss it to dogs. The woman's rebuttal was, "even the dogs under the table eat the children's crumbs" (Mark 7:28). This woman created a masterful word picture. I see children seated at a kitchen table eating lunch. Being children, they drop food on the floor. Under the table opportunistic dogs snap up dropped food. Jesus told the woman that because of her reply, her daughter was healed. The woman went home and found the demon gone from her daughter.

Attraction Power

Women can have power because they are attractive. Attraction is the ability to have someone like you.[1] Physical attraction encompasses being beautiful and winsome, but attraction is more than physical beauty. Attraction power is based on being authentic, often referred to as "being real." It encompasses being likeable. Often attractive women are described as "having a great personality." Generally, we are attracted to individuals who are similar to us. We associate with them more than individuals who are different. At church, I've noticed that same age-group individuals form relationships, sometimes even closed groups. That's because similar individuals reinforce each other's values, beliefs, and attitudes.

Attraction power is culture dependent.[1] Women can have attraction power in one culture, but not in another. A woman can only be attractive in a culture if she adapts and respects local customs and protocols. Queen Jezebel wasn't attractive to the Israelites. She was a product of Phoenicia (Tyre and Sidon). She didn't adapt herself to the Israelite culture which included the Israelite God.

Attractive women are better able to influence others. Attraction power creates a "halo effect." Researchers showed that highly attractive individuals were rated as being more effective speakers, more trustworthy, more supportive, and more encouraging of others.[1] They were viewed as friendly, social with strangers, and better listeners. In reality, attractive women may have had none of these attributes.

Charisma is an extraordinary amount of attraction power. Charisma draws people like a magnet. In the United States, some scientists asserted that individuals can be born with charisma. Charismatic individuals are positive, self-confident, energetic, and eloquent. Often they are assertive, charming, and present themselves well. Charismatic individuals appear accessible to others. Charisma can be used for good or ill.

I believe that Rebekah wasn't only physically attractive, but she was charismatic (Genesis chapter 24 and 27). At times, Rebekah used her charisma in beneficial ways; however, at times she used her charisma to harm others. Rebekah was Abraham's grandniece. In her childhood Rebekah lived in her father's home in Paddan Aram (Aram Naharaim). Abraham sent his servant, Eliezer, to Paddan Aram to obtain a wife for his son Isaac. After his long journey from Canaan to Paddan Aram, Eliezer rested at the town spring.

Rebekah arrived at the town spring carrying a clay water jar. The Bible described Rebekah as beautiful and an unmarried virgin (Genesis 24:15-16). Most likely she was in her mid-teens (13-16 years-of-age). Seeing a traveler (Eliezer) at the spring, Rebekah offered to draw water for him to drink. In the spirit of ancient Near East hospitality, Rebekah drew water for the ten camels in Eliezer's caravan. Not only was Rebekah beautiful, she was energetic and industrious. She extended herself to welcome a stranger whom she didn't know.

In Rebekah's home environment, she had power. Assertively, she invited Eliezer to her home without asking her parents or brother's permissions. Further, Rebekah's family bowed to her preference to leave immediately for Canaan to marry Isaac. After seeing Rebekah, Isaac loved and married her without delay.

Rebekah and Isaac had twins; the first-born was Esau and the second-born was Jacob. Rebekah loved Jacob more than Esau, even more than she loved Isaac. When old and eye sight dimmed, Isaac directed Esau to hunt for wild game, then to prepare a stew. Isaac loved stew made from wild meat. As Isaac and Esau shared a meal, Isaac planned to pass his paternal blessing to his first-born son. Rebekah overheard Isaac directions to Esau and cunningly devised an alternative plan. She instructed Jacob to bring her two choice young goats. She told Jacob that she would prepare a stew for Isaac from the goats that tasted just like wild game stew. Jacob could eat with Isaac and secure his father's blessing.

After Jacob heard Rebekah's plan, he pointed out that Esau's skin was hairy while his was smooth. If Isaac touched Jacob, Isaac would know that he wasn't Esau. Rebekah declared, "My son, …. just do what I say" (Genesis 27:13). Jacob spent his time around the campsite where he had daily contact with Rebekah. Rebekah's attraction, her history of putting Jacob first, and her strong, decisive character caused Jacob to obey his mother. Unfortunately, Rebekah used her charisma to harm, that is, to go against tradition and her husband's wishes.

The Israelites could have been thinking of Rebekah when they coined the proverb, "Charm is deceptive, and beauty is fleeting; but a woman who fears the LORD will be praised" (Proverbs 31:30).

Rebekah was attractive, charming, and charismatic. Her behavior showed that she loved herself, and probably Jacob, far more than she loved her husband or God. Many of Rebekah's actions weren't praiseworthy.

Not everyone that is physically attractive has high attraction power. For a woman to capitalize on her attractiveness, she must have personality traits that draw individuals to her. The New Testament and the Jewish historian, Josephus, had little good to say about Herodias, yet she was physically attractive. Probably, everyone who saw Herodias thought she was beautiful. Herodias was the wife of Herod Philip, a son of Herod the Great. On a visit to Philip, Herod Antipas saw Herodias. Whether or not Herod Antipas fell in love with Herodias wasn't clear, but he lusted for her.

Herod Antipas asked Herodias to marry him. At the time he was married to Phasaelis, the daughter of King Aretas IV of Nabataea. Nabataea was located south of Perea (Trans-Jordan), an area that Herod Antipas ruled. Herodias agreed to divorce Philip and marry Herod Antipas if he first divorced Phasaelis. Herod Antipas divorced his Nabatean princess and Herodias divorced Philip. The two of them married. Herodias went to live with Herod Antipas.

The result of Herod's lust/love for the beautiful Herodias was bloodshed. Aretas IV declared war on Herod Antipas. A battle ensued between Herod Antipas and Aretas's forces. Aretas won. Thousands of men were killed on both sides of the battle. Herodias was the perfect example why Christ warned not to judge by appearance (John 7:24). Herodias was beautiful; however, she was self-centered. She cared little who she harmed in the process of getting what she wanted.

Character Power

Character, a substantial personal power, is a person's usual traits or qualities. Character is part of a person's credibility. Character draws others, whether those others are family members, church friends, or work colleagues. Each of us wants to associate with highly credible people. We conclude rightly or wrongly that if we are friends with a person of good character, then we have good character. My minister has character power. He is knowledgeable and humble. Some days I even think that he is "holy." Secretly, I congratulate myself that I was smart enough to find Pastor Mark and his church. If bad character corrupts good character (1 Corinthians 15:33), perhaps my character will improve if I surround myself with individuals of good character like Pastor Mark.

A recognized expert in power, Bacon[1] averred that character is the only personal power source that can add or subtract from every other personal power source. A woman can be knowledgeable, attractive, and eloquent; but if she has character flaws, her power is diminished. Character flaws include being defensive, aloof, and volatile. A sense of entitlement, making destructive comments, and self-focus are character flaws.

While thinking about Bible woman that showed character power, I remembered the adage, "if you want to know a woman's character, look at her behavior." Then, I considered writing about the character power of Rizpah, Queen Ano, and Abigail. Finally, I settled on Jephthah's daughter as an example of a woman with character power. About now some of you are shaking your head and saying, "Never heard of her." I didn't know about Jephthah's daughter until several years ago when I wrote *Lesser Known Bible Characters*;[2] yet, this young woman had character power plus. How many daughters would tell their father to sacrifice her, essentially murder her, so the father could keep a rash vow to God? Jephthah's daughter did exactly that. Her story was set in the book of Judges. At no place was her name given; she was always referred to as Jephthah's daughter.

Jephthah was a judge in Gilead (Gad) east of the Jordan River. Before Jephthah led the Israelites into a major battle with the Ammonites, he promised that if God gave him victory, he would sacrifice whoever first exited his door when he returned home. After his victory, Jephthah returned home. His only child, a daughter, was the first individual out the door. She met her father dancing with tambourines. As soon as Jephthah saw his daughter, he remembered his vow. Jephthah tore his clothes and wailed his grief. He told his daughter the vow he made to God.

Jephthah's daughter could easily have gotten out of being sacrificed. First, she could have reminded her father that any sinful vow was not binding. Human sacrifice was an abomination to God and a sin (Deuteronomy 18:9-12). Second, rather than sacrifice her, Jephthah could have "given" her as a living sacrifice to God. As such, she would have remained unmarried throughout her life. Finally, Jephthah's daughter could have pleaded with her father not to sacrifice her. Jephthah loved his daughter, his only child. He would have tried hard—even risk being foresworn—to find a way out of this terrible predicament.

Instead of begging Jephthah to find an escape clause in his vow to God, Jephthah's daughter told him: "My father, you have opened your mouth to the Lord; do to me according to what has gone out of your mouth, now that the Lord has avenged you on your enemies, on the Ammonites.... Let this thing be done for me: leave me two months, that I may go up and down on the mountains and weep for my virginity, I and my companions" (Judges 11:36-37).

Although a mid-teen and a virgin, Jephthah's daughter had positive character traits. She had the courage to hold her father's feet to the fire and insist that he full-fill his vow to God. She revealed her humanity by asking for a two month reprieve to go into the mountains. A number of girlfriends went with her. They wanted to associate with a girl with such character strength. Jephthah's daughter's action set precedence in Israel. Thereafter, each year Israelite daughters went into the hills for four days to lament the daughter of Jephthah.

When the two months were over, Jephthah's daughter returned to her father to be sacrificed. Although Jephthah's daughter wept that she would never be a wife and have children, she didn't lash out at her father for his rash vow. She was restrained and temperate. She encouraged Jephthah to keep his vow even though it meant her death. She reminded her father that when he spoke the vow to God, other men heard him. If Jephthah didn't keep the vow, he would be foresworn before God and before his army. Perhaps, Jephthah's daughter knew something her father didn't, i.e., that a good name is more desirable than great riches (Proverbs 22:1). If Jephthah didn't keep his promise to God, he could have no credibility as a leader.

Unlike Bible writers who wrote chapters, even books, about the lives of Old Testament women, often New Testament writers recorded only snippets of information about them. In the New Testament Luke wrote briefly about Anna (Luke 2:33-35). Anna was a prophetess from the tribe of Asher, which was allocated land in the far northwest corner of the Promised Land. After she married, Anna lived with her husband seven years, then he died. When Luke introduced Anna she was approximately 84 years-of-age. Anna lived in the Woman's Court of the Jerusalem temple where day and night she fasted and prayed. The Women's Court was only about 200 square feet large. Can you imagine living in that small circumscribed space for 50 years? Anna did that.

Joseph and Mary brought baby Jesus to the Temple about 40 days after his birth to consecrate their first-born son to God. There, Anna saw the baby and knew immediately he was Israel's Messiah. God acknowledged Anna's devout character by allowing her to live to an old age and see the Christ child.

In many ways Jephthah's daughter and Anna were mirror opposites. One was at the beginning of her life and the other near the end. One was an Old Testament and the other a New Testament figure. One's story occurred in the frontier lands east of the Jordan River and the other in the Jerusalem temple. The story of Jephthah's daughter occurred over several chapters while Anna's is recorded in three short verses. In the Bible, documentation of women's character took many forms.

Relationship (History) Power

Between two people a relationship (a history) develops as they get to know each other over time, have positive experiences with each other, and disclose information about themselves. Usually, Bible women's relationships assumed trust. Trust developed as women saw how each other acted in different situations. Today, as we learn to know someone, we can increasingly predict their behavior; consequently, we feel safe around them. Coming into contact with another woman regularly, such as every day at the village well, moved a relationship forward faster than if the two women met only at annual religious festivals in Jerusalem.

Individuals from different cultures develop relationships at different speeds. In the United States individuals are more open and willing to form relationships rapidly. In other cultures, i.e., Japanese, Chinese, individuals move slower when developing a relationship.

Enduring human relationships among equals assumes reciprocity, that is, both women should be able to influence the other. Most women prefer to say "Yes" to a request from someone they know and like. Some relationship bonds aren't strong, such as my neighbor down the street. I wave to her as I drive past her home, but have never talked to her. If this neighbor asked me for a favor, I wouldn't feel constrained to say "Yes," particularly if it was inconvenient for me. Other relationship bonds, such as those in a family seem unbreakable. About forty years ago I baby sat my younger cousin, Julie. As an adult, I see Julie every two-to-three years, often at a funeral or wedding. On Facebook we are "friends," probably because we are family. Yet, if Julie called and needed a favor, I would say "Yes." I have confidence that Julie would do the same for me. Some relationships are strong because they are long-term.

Relationships and relationship power aren't static.[1] Consider a marriage: a husband and wife form a relationship based on their need for connectedness. If the need for connectedness of both spouses remains static, then the marriage relationship will proceed smoothly. Alternatively, over time one spouse may develop a need for autonomy stronger than the need for relational connectedness. When this happens, the marriage could end in divorce.

Potiphar was a wealthy Egyptian and possibly the commander of pharaoh's body guard.[3] He bought Joseph after Joseph was sold into slavery by his brothers and taken into Egypt (Genesis chapter 39). Over time Potiphar entrusted Joseph to care for everyone and everything in his household. The only person Potiphar didn't give Joseph control over was Potiphar's wife. Potiphar's wife was attractive, but self-centered. At one time she and Potiphar may have had a positive marriage relationship. Over time their relationship stagnated at best and devolved into both having affairs at worst.

Joseph was well built and handsome. During his duties as chief steward in Potiphar's house, he came into contact with Potiphar's wife. Potiphar's wife lusted for Joseph and brazenly tried to seduce him. Repeatedly, Joseph told her "No." Joseph didn't want to betray Potiphar or sin against God. Consider the power that Potiphar's wife possessed. She was beautiful. She was the wife of an estate owner whose husband had the ear of pharaoh. Despite her personal and positional power, Potiphar's wife couldn't seduce a slave. She became angry at Joseph and determined to get revenge on him. How could a lowly slave turn her down?

One day Potiphar's wife caught Joseph alone, grasped his cloak, and told him to come to bed with her. Joseph ran from her, leaving his cloak in her hands. Potiphar's wife told her husband that Joseph attacked her. When Potiphar heard his wife's story he was furious; however, the Bible doesn't say who Potiphar was furious at. Was it his wife or was it Joseph? I believe that Potiphar was angry at his wife, not Joseph.

True, Potiphar put Joseph in prison; however, Potiphar could have easily had Joseph killed. A slave who attack a high ranking Egyptian woman deserved death. As the chief of Pharaoh's body guard, Potiphar possessed sufficient power that killing one Israelite slave, even an innocent one, would have caused no push back in Egyptian society.

Potiphar had a long term relationship with his wife. He knew her every weakness, i.e., beauty, self-centeredness, vindictiveness. Potiphar had a shorter relationship with Joseph; yet, he saw how honorably Joseph full-filled his duties. Potiphar didn't believe his wife was innocent. Perhaps, he believed little, if any, of her story. His own pride and the need to show support for his Egyptian wife required Potiphar to take action against Joseph. That action was to put Joseph in an Egyptian prison, rather than to kill him.

The New Testament tells the story of another husband and wife, Ananias and Sapphira (Acts 5:1-11). Although a marriage can bring out the best in each spouse, a long spousal relationship can bring out the worst traits in each, as they did with Ananias and Sapphira. Their story was set in Jerusalem in the early church (Acts 5:1-11). The

Bible didn't record Ananias and Sapphira ages. Likely, they were middle-aged and married long enough to acquire some wealth and property. Definitely, they were married long enough to understand each other's strengths and weaknesses.

At this time, church members shared all possessions. From time-to-time, a person who owned lands or houses sold them and brought the money to the apostles. The money was distributed to anyone in the church who had need. Ananias sold some property. With Sapphira's full knowledge, Ananias brought only a portion of the profit to the apostles. The Holy Spirit disclosed to Peter that Ananias only gave a portion of the selling price to the church. Peter confronted Ananias with his duplicity. Ananias fell down and died in fear of Peter's accusation.

About three hours later, Sapphira entered the church group. She was unaware of what happened to Ananias. Peter asked Sapphira if the selling price of the land was what Ananias gave the church. Sapphira said "Yes," thus, she too lied to Peter. Hearing Sapphira's lie, Peter asked her how she could conspire (with Ananias) to test the Holy Spirit. Then, Peter told her that the men who buried Ananias would bury her also. Sapphira fell down and died.

When Ananias gave a portion of the selling price of the property to the Jerusalem church, Sapphira went along with her husband's duplicity. Sapphira and Ananias were equally culpable. When God created Eve, she was to be Adam's help mate or helper in the same way that the Holy Spirit helps Christians. Sapphira failed in her God-assigned role. If she was really Ananias's help mate, she would have cautioned, rather than abet, his choice to lie to the church.

Conclusion

Expressive (eloquence) power gave more clout than any other personal power source. The gap between the overall influence ratings of a woman with high expressiveness versus low expressiveness scores was wider than for any other personal power source. Because Ruth was eloquent, we remember her as a powerful Bible woman. Knowledge power was second only to expressiveness in the impact it had on a woman's capacity to influence others.[1]

Women who had high knowledge power were three times more influential than those with low knowledge power.

The importance attached to attractiveness varies in different countries. Probably 3000 years ago, Israelites rated attraction as highly important. A woman's character can add or subtract from every other personal power source.[1] Attraction and relationship power and attraction and character power were highly correlated. Although different—attraction, relationship, and character— formed a constellation of personal power sources. At the same time, if a woman had high attraction and relationship powers, but she had character flaws, her power and influence were diminished greatly.

Relationship power doesn't require admiration from other persons; however, it does require acceptance.[1] A Bible woman's power over and ability to influence another person increased with both the length and strength of the relationship. Relationship power diminished when something disturbing or repugnant was learned about a woman.

Chapter 2

Positional Power Sources

Bible women had personal power—knowledge, eloquence, relationships, attraction, and character—and they had positional power. For Bible women, positional power resulted from their roles, resources they controlled, networks they were part of, information they accessed or retrieved, and their reputations. In the ancient Near East, the power of a wife over family decisions was substantial. No matter how much Jacob wanted out of Paddan Aram and away from his father-in-law, he didn't finalize his plans to leave the country until he had agreement from his wives (Genesis 31:4-16).

In the Old Testament a wife controlled household resources. Often she had information and networks that men didn't have. The New Testament contained several examples of women business owners and women who managed their own money. A married woman with a good community reputation was valued by her husband and children. Her reputation enhanced her husband's reputation (Proverbs chapter 31). On the other hand, fathers cautioned sons to avoid woman with poor reputations (Proverbs 7:6-27). Husbands, children, and communities rejected adulterous or immoral women (Hosea 2:1-10); often their reputations were irreparable.

Role Power

The power of a Bible woman's role cannot be over-estimated. Frequently the Bible identified women by their role in the family, i.e., Deborah was the wife of Lippidoth, Rizpah the daughter of Aiah. At other times Bible women were identified by their clan, tribe, or nation. Examples include that Naomi was an Ephrathite, Manoah's wife from the tribe of Dan, and Ruth was a Moabite. Occasionally, a woman was associated with a town or city. A witch lived in Endor, a town in Manasseh. Lydia was from Thyatira, a town in Asia Minor.

Role power was one of the strongest power sources that a Bible woman had. Reasons were that a woman with a high role position, be it wife, queen, or judge, could reward or punish individuals under her; thus, she could coerce certain behaviors from these individuals.[1]

In the Bible, particularly before the Israelite monarch and its accompanying bureaucracy, much of a woman's role power came from her position in the family. An example was the wife of the very wealthy Abraham. Sarah abused her slave Hagar so badly that Hagar fled the camp (Genesis 16:6); yet, Sarah wasn't held accountable for her abuse.

Often Bible women wielded power based on a family relationship, but that power didn't extend beyond the family. For example, Caleb had a soft spot for his daughter Acsah (Joshua 15:16-19). Because of the Caleb-Acsah relationship, Acsah had power over her father. Caleb found Acsah a strong husband. He granted valuable land and water to the newly-weds when Acsah asked for them. At the same time, Acsah had little or no power in the new nation of Israel or even in her tribe (Judah).

The strength of role power is in group social norms coupled with individual tendency to conform to the norms.[1] Social norms asserted that a superior could tell or ask a follower to do something, as long as the demand was within the scope of the superior's authority. In the Bible a title was a badge of authority that assured compliance from subordinates. Bible titles were different than in the 21st century. Common Bible titles were mother, wife, prophetess, and queen. A daughter accepted that her mother could direct her to grind meal. A servant conformed to her mistress's desire, i.e., Rachel's maid servant, Bilhah, complied with Rachel's direction that she becomes Jacob's concubine (Genesis 30:3-6). Queen Ano obeyed her husband and king's direction to disguise herself as a poor woman and seek information about her son's health from the prophet Ahijah (1 Kings 14:1-5).

Generally, role power operated within a certain area or sphere, and was non-existent outside of that area. Puah and Shiphrah were noted midwives in Egypt before the Exodus (Exodus 1:15-16). If either told an Israelite woman to take some precaution to prevent a miscarriage, most likely the Israelite woman followed their recommendation. At the same time, if Puah or Shiphrah told an Israelite man how to heal whip lash damage to his back, the man could discount the midwife's advice. In the latter instance, the midwife gave advice outside her knowledge field.

Part of me wants to say that role-related authority was stronger in Bible times than in the 21st century. Yet, Miriam challenged Moses' role as leader of the Israelite nation about 1800 BC (Numbers 12:1-2). In the wilderness, Israelites murmured, some even rebelled, against Moses' authority (Numbers chapter 14). Perhaps role-related authority was always uncertain and could be challenged.

High role power was correlated closely with assertiveness, behaving self-confidently, using a compelling tone of voice, and using authority without being heavy-handed.[1] In the New Testament 2000 years ago, Mary, Jesus, and his disciples were guests at a wedding. The host ran out of wine which was an insult to guests and embarrassment to the host. Assertively, Mary (Jesus's mother) took command in this disastrous situation. She directed wedding servants "Do whatever he tells you" (John 2.5), referring to whatever Jesus told them to do. Servants obeyed Mary even though she was not the master of the banquet because she was confident in this situation. Mary had a plan to right this wrong when no one else took action.

Frequently, role power depended on obtaining consent from the governed or individuals who received direction. High role power of the type, "do it because I say so," often got compliance but little commitment from followers. If role power was abused consistently, so that governed people became agitated, role power was reduced and resistance mounted.[1] An example of a woman who lost her role power was Queen Athaliah (2 Kings 11:1-20). Athaliah was the only queen who ruled Judah. She was the daughter of King Ahab and Queen Jezebel of Israel. Her marriage to King Jehoram of Judah formed a political alliance between the two countries. Athaliah built a temple to Baal in Jerusalem and introduced Baal worship in Judah. After her son, King Ahaziah, was murdered, Athaliah killed his children, that is, her own grandchildren. Then, she declared herself Queen of Judah.

One of Ahaziah's sons, Joash, was saved. Jehoiada, high priest in Solomon's temple, hid Joash in a temple bedroom from about age one until he was seven years-old. Then, Jehoiada staged a coup against Queen Athaliah. Joash was declared king in the Jerusalem temple. Representatives from towns and villages throughout Judah attended Joash's coronation, as did military commanders who stood in the temple in support of Joash. Levite choirs played musical instruments, sang, and led the people in psalms. Trumpets sounded. A lost son of the house of David lived! When Athaliah heard the noise, she went to God's temple. Immediately, she knew what was happening. Passionately, Queen Athaliah tore her robes and shouted, "Treason, Treason." The chief priest, Jehoiada, ordered military commanders to kill Athaliah.

Planning and organizing a coup against Queen Athaliah took months. Yet, no one in Judah divulged the seditious information to the queen. No one resisted the change in Judah's regent; not even Athaliah's personal body guards who were hired to defend her. Because of her ruthless actions, Athaliah lost her moral authority in the nation of Judah. Citizens no longer consented to have Queen Athaliah rule them. Role alone couldn't make Queen Athaliah sufficiently inspiring and compelling to keep her throne.

In the New Testament, Lois lived with her daughter Eunice. Lois and Eunice were both Jewish women; however, only a few Jewish families live in their town (Lystra). While Lois' husband lived, she had role power in that she managed his household. When Lois' husband died, Lois' role power as his wife disappeared. Her husband's estate went to a male relative. Lois had no son to care for her needs and her grandson (Timothy) was too young to establish his own household. Lois had no male relatives where she could take control of a household. Probably, Lois had scant family network apart from her daughter, Eunice. Eunice married a Greek man (Acts 16:1; 2 Timothy 1:5). Although Lois lived with Eunice, she had no role power in the household.

Resource Power

Bible women had power through the resources they controlled. Primarily, these resources included food supplies and allocation of work to servants and slaves; however, a few Old Testament women owned land as in the cases of Zelophehad's daughters (Numbers 27:1-11) and the idealized wife (Proverbs 31:16). In the New Testament some women had their own money. A New Testament woman headed a business, i.e., Lydia (Acts 16:11-15).

Scarcity is the key to resource power. To have resource power, someone must want the resources a woman owned, possessed, or controlled. Often high role power and high resource power went hand-in-hand. When a Bible woman was in a high position (role), she controlled more resources. Research today showed that women with high resource power tended to be insensitive to other's feelings and needs.[1] At times, they had little insight into what others valued. Individuals with high resource power had difficulty building close relationships. They were unable to resolve conflicts and disagreements.

As I studied the Bible to find individuals with high resource power, I came to the story of Abigail (1 Samuel chapter 25). It included each component of resource power; that is, having, needing, and supplying resources. Further, a woman was the heroine of the story. Abigail's husband Nabal was a wealthy farmer. Nabal owned 3000 sheep and 1000 goats which he pastured near Carmel. Although assertive, Nabal was the Bible prototype of a resource-rich person who lacked interpersonal skills. The Bible recorded that Nabal was harsh and behaved badly. The evolving story of Nabal's behavior supported this conclusion.

David and about 600 men hid from King Saul in the Carmel area. David needed food and supplies to sustain his followers. Yet, at no time did David or his men steal even one of Nabal's livestock. Just the opposite, David protected both flocks and herders. When Nabal was sheering his sheep, normally a time of joy and sharing, David sent men to Nabal and asked for food. David had every expectation that Nabal would share his resources with men who protected his flocks. Shockingly, Nabal refused to give food to David's men. Nabal even insulted David's men who made the request to him. When David heard about Nabal's actions, he was furious! David ordered his men to get ready for battle, i.e., to strap on their swords. David and 400 men started for Nabal's home. David was determined to kill every male in Nabal's household.

Because of her position as Nabal's wife, Abigail controlled resources, particularly food supplies. Although some married couples are similar, Abigail and Nabal were diametrical opposites. Abigail was beautiful, discerning, intelligent, and articulate. When a servant told Abigail about Nabal's treatment of David's men, she was appalled. She understood how angry David would be because of Nabal's rude refusal of resources. Immediately, Abigail gathered food—bread, wine, prepared sheep, parched grain, raisins, and fig cakes. Without telling Nabal, Abigail put the food on donkeys and went out to meet David and his men. When Abigail encountered David, she abased herself and begged him to accept her gifts of food for himself and his followers. Abigail pleaded with David not to kill the members of Nabal's homestead. David accepted the supplies. He thanked Abigail for the food and drink for his men. David even thanked Abigail for preventing him from attacking Nabal's home.

Nabal, Abigail, and David had resource power even though they were different types of resources. Both Nabal and Abigail had food which David needed. David had followers willing to protect Nabal's herders and flocks, but also willing to kill the men of Nabal's household. Nabal and David should have been able to exchange resources to the benefit of both; however, that didn't happen. Seemingly, Nabal didn't see the wisdom of, or know how, to build mutually beneficial relationships. Thank God for Abigail or every person in Nabal's household would have been killed!

Bacon's research showed that individuals with high resource power tended to rate low on attraction power.[1] For some reason control of substantial resources made a person unattractive and possibly unlikable. Nabal's behavior exemplified Bacon's finding about attraction and control of resources; however, Abigail was an exception to Bacon's findings. She was attractive and knew how to manage resources. In fact, Abigail was so attractive and intelligent that David married her after Nabal died.

In the New Testament, a number of women traveled with Jesus over his three-year ministry. They supported Jesus and his disciples from their own money. These women were Mary Magdalene; Joanna, the wife of Chuza who was the manager of Herod Antipas's household; Suzanna; Salome, mother of the apostles James and John; Mary who was Jesus's mother; and another Mary who was the mother of James the younger and Joseph (Luke 8:1-3, 24:10; Mark 15:40, 16:1). Jesus accepted physical support, that is, food, money, clothes, from these women. With the possible exception of Salome, the mother of James and John, the women didn't expect anything from Jesus in return for their support.

Information Power

Bible women gained information power by accessing, interpreting, and disseminating information. They accessed or retrieved information (pieces of data) from family, neighbors, visitors, and merchants in the marketplace. At times, God talked to women, i.e., Manoah's wife and Huldah.

As I pondered Bible women's access to information, intuitively, I thought women had less information access than men. In reality, women may have had equal access to information. At times information that women and men wanted was the same; but, they used it differently. For example, both Bible women and men wanted information on crop yields. A woman's concern was feeding members of her household. A man wanted the information to decide which crops to plant in his own fields or how to feed soldiers if he went to war. At other times Bible women wanted different information than men. A woman wanted information on dyes to color fabrics, while a man wanted information on the best way to make bronze or iron farm implements or weapons.

Not all information was equal. Some information was irrelevant; no one wanted or needed it. Retrieving such information was not value-added and wasted time and energy. Scarce, but needed, information was valuable. Having scarce information increased a woman's power. Whether plentiful or scarce, all information a woman used had to be accurate. In the ancient Near East, traders, travelers, and even wise men could have outdated or just wrong information. Using and sharing incorrect information ruined a woman's credibility.

Although information power began with access to the right data, correctly interpreting information was important. Interpreting information (pieces of data) was one of the greatest ways to build information power. Currently, the worldwide web and published articles contain huge amounts of information. At times it is difficult to select the right information from all that is available. A Bible woman who wanted information power had to access correct information, then organize and interpret the sundry data points. In the process of organizing and interpreting data, women included some and discarded other data points. A Bible woman constantly asked herself, "What relevance (if any) does that piece of information have to my goals?"

Consider a Jerusalem-based Bible woman who wanted to make linen garments for family members (Proverbs 31: 22-24). She needed to know if Egyptian flax harvest was good or bad. Flax yield in Egypt influenced the cost of linen thread or cloth in Jerusalem. Were seasonal storms on the eastern Mediterranean Sea worse than normal? If so, a percent of ships carrying flax to Joppa (the port for Jerusalem) could have been lost. Were there problems getting linen thread the approximate thirty miles between Joppa and Jerusalem, i.e., increased numbers of robbers on the road? Did rains destroy normally passable roads? Was there a health epidemic anywhere along the flax/linen route that reduced flow of flax/linen between Egypt and Jerusalem? Was the woman able to hire household servants who could weave linen thread into cloth? The information needed by this woman was multifaceted and made a substantial difference in household management.

Importantly, Bible women were identified as having information power only when they shared (disseminated) the information with the right people at the right time.[1] Princess Michal loved David before he was king over Israel. King Saul saw Michal's love and arranged a marriage between David and Michal. Saul hoped that he could use David and Michel's marriage to access and kill David. At one point King Saul sent men to Michal and David's home in the evening. King Saul ordered the watching men to kill David the following morning.

Somehow Michal learned of the plan. Perhaps one of Michal's palace friends told her about King Saul's order. Perhaps, Michal saw men outside her home and recognized them as her father's assassins. Michal interpreted the information and told David, "If you don't run for your life tonight, tomorrow you will be killed" (1 Samuel 19:11). Then, Michal helped David escape through a window. As predicted, Saul's men entered David's home the next morning to kill him. By putting snippets of information from a variety of sources together, Michal was able to draw the correct conclusion and David escaped King Saul's murderous plan.

In the New Testament, Mary Magdalene had information power. She was the first person to encounter Jesus after he rose from the grave (John 20:10-18). Mary went to the disciples with the good news. She told them all the things Jesus said to her in their brief encounter in the garden. Can you imagine what would have happened if Mary went silent; if she saw the risen Jesus, but told no one about her encounter? The disciples would have continued in their pain. They wouldn't have believed the two disciples who returned from Emmaus, enthusiastic about their encounter with the risen Jesus. Today in Christian circles, Mary Magdalene is named "the apostle to the apostles" because she the first person to take the good news of the risen Jesus to the apostles.

Network Power

Other women and occasionally men were part of a Bible woman's network. Network power was, and is today, connections to others. Bible women communicated ideas and expertise (how to do tasks) to network connections. Even before the advent of electronic and written communications, there were women who were "connectors." They seemed to know everyone else.

Networks are ties between people who live, work, and socialize together. Bible women's strongest networks were people they knew best and communicated with most often. Examples included (a) a woman's mother and mother-in-law particularly if the mother-in-law lived with the woman's husband; (b) children, sisters, and sisters-in-law; and (c) extended family members such as cousins or cousin's wives.

Although strong network relationships were important to Bible women, so were large numbers of weak network relationships. Weak network ties provided women with information and resources beyond those available in their own family circle. An example of a Bible woman's weak network connection could be another woman she talked with only at annual festivals in Jerusalem. Weak network individuals were important,[1] particularly if they helped a woman achieve her objectives, i.e., getting flax thread for clothes or unique spices for cooking. The old adage about success depending less on "what you knew and more on whom you knew" was true in relation to Bible women's network power.

Most Bible women's networks were informal. The basis of these informal networks was a mutual interest in staying in touch. Bible women remained interested in other women over decades of time. Mary lived in Nazareth, Galilee and an older cousin, Elizabeth, lived in the hill country (Hebron) of Judah; yet, they kept in contact with one another (Luke 1:39-45). Mary went to stay with Elizabeth shortly after she learned that she was pregnant.

Often network power didn't exist on its own. Rather, network power emerged from the joint strength of other power sources, i.e., role, resources, information, knowledge, and attraction. Network power was often transitory. It could be lost if a woman (a) refused to reciprocate once a favor was done for her, (b) moved out of a role, or (c) did something so repugnant that individuals no longer wanted to be associated with her. On occasion a Bible woman's resources and information diminished or dried up entirely, the result was that she lost network power.

Among Bible women, Huldah had network power (2 Chronicles 34:22-28). Huldah was a prophetess who lived in Jerusalem at the time of King Josiah (640-609 BC). Josiah attempted to turn Judah from idolatry back to God worship. In the process of repairing the temple, the Book of Law was discovered. When the Book was read to Josiah, he was devastated. He believed that God's righteous anger would fall on Judah because the nation rejected God and turned to idol worship. King Josiah ordered his top officials to ask God what would happen to him, Judah, and the remnant of Israel.

The officials, to include the temple high priest, went to a woman prophetess, Huldah. Huldah was well-connected. Her husband, Shallum, was the keeper of the temple wardrobe. Writers speculated that Shallum was Josiah's teacher/mentor when Josiah was a child. Huldah lived in a college, called a house of doctrine. At this time in Judah history, possibly, Jeremiah and Habbakuk were in Jerusalem. Despite the presence of these two esteemed prophets, Josiah's officials sought out Huldah. They may have believed, or at least hoped, that Huldah would give a softer or more favorable interpretation of God's pending wrath on Judah.

As a true prophetess, Huldah spoke God's words. Because prophets and prophetess declared God's exact words, Jeremiah, Habbakuk, and Huldah would have had the same interpretation for King Josiah's delegation. Huldah's response began with "This is what the Lord, the God of Israel says" (2 Chronicles 34:23). God planned to bring disaster on Jerusalem and its people—all the curses written in the Book of Law—because Judah rejected him and worshiped other gods. Because King Josiah's heart was responsive to the Book of Law and because Josiah humbled himself before God, God would wait to destroy Jerusalem until after Josiah died.

In the New Testament, Martha and Mary of Bethany were two women with network power. In contrast to Huldah who had a formal network because of her position, Martha and Mary had an informal one. Martha and Mary lived with their brother, Lazarus, in Bethany, a small town about two miles outside of Jerusalem. They had wealth (Mark 14:3-9); however, wealth wasn't the reason for their network power. Their network power came from close family ties plus friendship with Jesus. When Jesus was in the Jerusalem area, often he and his disciples stayed in Lazarus's home. The two sisters prepared and served meals to Jesus and his disciples. Lazarus, Martha, and Mary loved Jesus. They believed that Jesus was the Messiah; further, Jesus loved them (John 11:5). There was nothing formal about the network between the family and Jesus.

Lazarus got very sick and his sisters sent for Jesus. Somehow they knew Jesus was across the Jordan River in an area that John the Baptist once frequented. The sisters believed their friend Jesus could and would heal Lazarus. Deliberately, Jesus didn't come to the family's home until Lazarus was in the tomb for four days. When Jesus arrived in Bethany, he met each sister separately. Each had the same tearful message—if you would have been here, Lazarus wouldn't have died (John 11:21, 32). Jesus was so distraught by their tears and sadness that he too wept. Then, Jesus called Lazarus out of his burial tomb. Martha and Mary used their friendship (network power) to summon Jesus to them and to influence Jesus to raise Lazarus from the dead.

Reputation Power

Reputation was one of the most important power sources a Bible woman had. Reputation power existed in relation to other people. It was what others thought about the woman. Bible women with good (high) reputations were able to build rapport and trust with other women and even with men. They used authority without appearing heavy-handed. A good reputation is "a rising tide that lifts all boats."[1] In other words, a good reputation made a Bible woman appear better and more skilled in every way.

A woman's reputation was a group consensus, a shared opinion, of her value or merit.[1] A person in power or at the nexus of a large network of individuals could disproportionately influence a woman's reputation. If a powerful individual said good things about a woman, the good information spread and her reputation power increased. In Proverbs the ideal wife was lauded by her husband's colleagues (Proverbs 31:23). Her community reputation was stellar. Centrally-located or powerful individuals could reduce a woman's reputation power. I've seen a mere lift of an eyebrow or grimace from a leader cause a woman's organizational reputation to plummet.

Reputation was a factor that decided a woman's effectiveness at influencing others. Women with a better (higher power) reputation had more influence than those with a poorer (lower power) reputation. When I pondered women with high reputation power in the Old Testament, my mind went to the Witch of Endor. She was a Canaanite woman who was reputed to contact dead spirits.

Before a major battle with the Philistines, King Saul ordered his men to find a witch who could communicate with the dead. King Saul wanted to consult with the dead prophet Samuel about the pending battle. Probably, King Saul's order puzzled his men because early in his reign, Saul expelled mediums and spiritualists from the Promised Land. Likely, "expel" was a euphemism for killing them as Mosaic Law required. Notice, this Canaanite woman's reputation power wasn't good in the sense that she was a "good" woman; rather her reputation was good in that it identified her as powerful.

A disguised King Saul went to the witch of Endor's home. He asked her to bring up Samuel's spirit, so Saul could consult with Samuel.

The witch brought up Samuel's spirit; but Samuel wasn't happy to be there! Samuel told Saul that the Israelites would lose the upcoming battle and Saul would be killed. Can you imagine the magnitude of the witch of Endor's reputation power after this event? Not only did she bring up the dead Samuel's spirit, but every word spoken by Samuel came true. King Saul and several of his sons were killed in the battle with the Philistines.

According to the Bible "A good name is better than precious ointment" (Ecclesiastes 7:1). A good name, as evidenced by a good reputation, was a precious asset; but it took time to build. A Bible woman had to live and work in a place for people to note her character. In ancient times, a woman's reputation often preceded her in the community. That reputation was relayed through gossip and resulted from praise or criticism by others. Earlier, I identified Ruth's expressive power when she refused to leave Naomi. Yet, Ruth had more than eloquence. After Naomi and Ruth returned to the Bethlehem area, Ruth gleaned in the fields to provide grain for her mother-in-law. She developed a reputation as a hard worker in the Bethlehem community. Ruth's hard work was noted by farmers in the area (Ruth 2:11-12), one of whom was Boaz who both admired and married Ruth.

To some extent reputation is predicated on cultural values and the social norms of a community. At the same time, universal character strengths existed that could enhance a woman's reputation. Courage and the ability to overcome fear were valued in every culture. In Jericho, Rahab was a prostitute. No one described her as having a "good" reputation in the traditional sense; yet, Rabab was one of the most admired women in the Bible. Despite Rahab's fear, she hid two Israelite spies and lied to the king of Jericho about them (Joshua chapter 2). This same Rahab married Salmon and was an ancestor of Christ (Matthew 1:5).

Reputation reflected and reinforced social norms, socially desirable behaviors, and attitudes.[1] If a woman behaved differently from the community's social norms, she lost her good reputation and any reputation power she possessed. In the Bible often a Bible woman's reputation depended on her morality. A prime example was Gomer, Hosea's wife (Hosea chapters 1 and 3). Hosea and Gomer lived in Israel during the reign of Jeroboam II. Hosea was God's prophet.

When God directed Hosea to marry an adulterous woman, he married Gomer. In ancient Israel, often kinship regulated marriage. Possibly, Gomer was a cousin or second cousin to Hosea. Relative or not, marriage to a harlot brought shame on Hosea's entire family.

Marriage could have restored some of Gomer's reputation; however, during the marriage Gomer was sexually unfaithful to Hosea. Gomer believed that other men could give her more physical comforts and ornaments than Hosea. She left Hosea and abandoned their three children. At this point Gomer's reputation got even worse than it was before her marriage to Hosea.

Over time working as a prostitute palled. Gomer realized that her life as Hosea's wife was better than her current life. Possibly, Gomer lost her looks or her freshness. Unthinking or uncaring that she embarrassed Hosea, Gomer asked him if she could return to his house. Hosea refused. Gomer became destitute. She sold herself into slavery to have a place to live and food to eat. Eventually, God directed Hosea to purchase Gomer from the slave owner (Hosea 3:1).

It was possible to rebuild a reputation after it was tarnished, but the rebuilding process took time.[1] To rebuild a reputation a woman must first own up to her mistakes. Second, the woman must show she learned from her mistakes and perform better in the future. Something about Gomer's initial request to return to Hosea's home didn't ring true, because Hosea said "No." Later when Hosea bought Gomer from slavery, he provided clear boundaries for their life together. Neither spouse could have sex outside of the marriage. Only after Gomer proved her loyalty, would Hosea resume sexual relations with her. Because Hosea resumed a marriage relationship with Gomer didn't mean that her reputation in her community was restored. Very possibly Gomer's reputation was so tarnished that it was never restored.

Conclusion

Having high role power versus low role power doubled a woman's ability to influence others;[1] yet, high role power wasn't as important as personal (expressiveness, knowledge, reputation, attraction or characters) powers. Role power was highest in countries that historically were more hierarchical and where rank and position were more important, i.e., southeastern Asia. Examining Bible history and culture caused me to conclude that role power was more important in the Bible era than it is now.

Resource power, the weakest of all power sources, was often tied to information power.[1] In the Bible era, individuals valued social networks. Social networks were sources of information. Social networks were present in every culture. Having large social networks could triple a woman's ability to influence others. Israelites valued networks. Even today, of the many countries where social network power was studied, Israel ranked highest in network power.

Two personal power sources (knowledge and expressiveness) and two organizational power sources (resource and network) were correlated with a woman's reputation. Personal knowledge correlated the highest with reputation power; while resource power correlated the lowest with reputation power. This latter finding suggested that women with a good reputation were viewed as powerful even if they did not control a large amount of resources.

Chapter 3

Will Power

Will power comes from within. It begins with a desire to be powerful and moves to a determination to make a difference. It comes from a woman's dreams plus her drive to achieve those dreams. Will power is more than desire, will power is action. In the Bible some women were victims such as Jacob's daughter, Dinah, and David's daughter, Princess Tamar. Other women took their lives into their own hands. Bible women with will power had courage to act and to persist even in the face of opposition and failure.

Nothing great was ever created aside from will power.[1] Walt Whitman called will power "personal force." According to Whitman, character and personal force were the only investment worth making. In the late 20th and early 21st century, personal will power wasn't a popular notion. Some social scientists no longer believed will power existed. Will power wasn't included in many personality theories. Philosophers spoke and wrote about freedom of action rather than the power of the will. McNair[4] disagreed with these modern views of will power. He wrote: "No will means no capacity for making moral choices. No will means no responsibility for sin. Faults and shortcomings can be blamed on genetics, background, parents, environment, or just "bad luck." The "non-existence of the will" theory is just another way for a confused and deceived mankind to pursue its lusts without the pain of guilt and shame."

God said that will power is crucial for success in life. In the Bible, will power was often called "self-control." The Bible declared that will power and self-control were from God, i.e., God gave us a spirit not of fear, but of power, love, and self-control (2 Timothy 1:7). King Solomon wrote that an individual without self-control was like a city with broken down walls (Proverbs 25:28). I think this verse means that without self-control or will power, we are open to the ravages of temptation and sin. Gaining control of the will was and is crucial to inner peace and success. Ultimately, self-control allowed Bible women to use their energies to advance God's plan both for them and for mankind.

Every time I think of a Bible woman with will power, I think of Tamar, Judah's daughter-in-law (Genesis chapter 38). Judah married a Canaanite woman and they had three sons, Er, Onan, and Shelah. When Er reached adulthood, Judah obtained a wife for him. Her named was Tamar; she was a Canaanite. Er died. Following ancient marriage customs, Tamar became the wife of Onan. Onan died also. The Bible recorded that both Er and Onan died because they were wicked; however, Judah feared that Tamar was some type of "black widow." Judah sent Tamar back to her father's house. Judah said that when Shelah grew older, Tamar would become his wife. When Shelah reached adulthood, Judah didn't contact Tamar so she could marry Shelah. Tamar's childless state left her socially and financially disadvantaged. In the ancient Near East, a son cared for his mother after the father's death. Often the mother lived with the eldest son.

Judah's wife died and sometime later Judah went to shear his sheep. Hirah, a long-time friend, went with Judah. On the way Judah came to Enaim. There, Judah saw a veiled woman. Believing she was a shrine prostitute, Judah propositioned her. He agreed to pay her a young goat in exchange for sexual intercourse. Because Judah had no goat with him, he left his seal, cord, and staff with the woman. Judah told the woman that the next day he would send her a goat and reclaim the symbols of his clan and individual identity. The next day Hirah took the goat to Enaim, but he couldn't find the prostitute. From townsmen, Hirah learned that Enaim never had a shrine prostitute. Hirah went back and told Judah the full story. Afraid that he would be ridiculed if he continued the search for a non-existent prostitute, Judah gave up his seal, cord, and staff.

About three months later, Judah heard that Tamar was pregnant. Judah ordered that Tamar be burned to death because her pregnancy was evidence that she prostituted herself. Before she could be punished, Tamar sent Judah his seal, cord, and staff. Tamar told Judah that she was pregnant by the man who owned the identity symbols. Judah recognized his own symbols and didn't have Tamar killed. Tamar birthed twins, Perez and Zerah. Judah, Tamar, and their son, Perez, were ancestors of Jesus. Tamar saw a future for herself that didn't include abject poverty. Through her will power, she achieved that future.

A Bible woman's will power originated inside of her; will power wasn't imposed from outside. Bible women's will power encompassed their beliefs, desires, motivations, and importantly, actions. Will power is unique to an individual. A Bible woman's will power could overcome a myriad of disadvantages, such as being born a slave or inadequate resources. Will power isn't determined by culture. In the Bible some Canaanite, Israelite, Egyptian, Midianite, etc., women possessed will power and others didn't. Will power came from a Bible woman's courage and an unwillingness to be defeated. Will power was demonstrated when a Bible woman acted to change a situation.

As much as I deplore the actions of Lot's daughters, they were two women who exhibited great will power. The daughter's story was recorded in the 19th chapter of Genesis, showing that even early in Bible history, women had will power. After Lot and his two daughters escaped Sodom, they went to a small town named Zoar (Genesis 19:30). Later, Lot was afraid to remain in Zoar. He took his two daughters to live in a mountain cave. The Bible doesn't tell readers how long Lot and his daughters lived there; but eventually, the daughters talked about who would provide for them after their father died. In the ancient Near East, fathers were responsible for finding husbands for daughters; however, after the destruction of Sodom, Lot made no effort to secure husbands for his daughters.

Lot's daughters developed a plan to secure their future. On separate nights, a daughter got Lot drunk and raped him. Both became pregnant by their father. We can safely infer that if a first rape didn't result in a pregnancy, the girls had sex with Lot a second or third time. Both pregnancies resulted in sons, Moab (father of the Moabites) and Ben-Ammi (father of the Ammonites). If a pregnancy resulted in female offspring, the daughters would have raped Lot again. The daughters' actions were morally depraved. The best that can be said of them is that they saw a problem and solved it.

Ideally, a Bible woman's will power was grounded in obedience to God and a desire to please God (Isaiah 1:19). Certainly a Bible woman, like a 21st century woman, had to pray that God would teach her his ways; and, more importantly, God would give her a desire to do what God had in mind for her life (Psalm 40:8).

Because action is part of will power, a Bible woman could lessen her own power of will. For example, a Bible woman could decide that she would stay silent in the face of opposition, such as a heavy-handed father or husband. If a woman made a decision not to act, her desire to make a change probably continued; but, she consciously rejected taking any action. Because will power includes action, when a Bible woman didn't act, her will power was reduced or sublimated. Very likely, few women who consciously set aside their will power were described in the Bible. Importantly, every desire a Bible woman had wasn't from God. Some desires came from Satan. Writing to the church at Rome, Paul cautioned that women (and men) needed to test their desires to discern if they were from God (Romans 12:2). God-given desires were good, acceptable, and perfect.

God actively condemned some women's actions even when those actions came from a woman's will power. An example was the magician-prophetesses described by Ezekiel (Ezekiel 13:17-23). Apparently, the women were Israelites who associated with each other in a guild-type arrangement. God accused the false prophetesses of ensnaring souls of Israelites by having them tie magic charms around their wrists and wear magic veils. At this time in Israel, there were so many magician-prophetesses selling charms that charms were cheap to buy.

An Israelite's primary relationship was to be with God. Most assuredly, true prophetesses had to stay close to God to ascertain what God wanted them to say. These magician-prophetesses didn't do that. They profaned God's name by claiming they received visions from him, when they didn't. Their visions were either a product of their own imaginations, or given by dark powers. Often the magician-prophetesses primary relationship was with Satan or one of his minions.

God asked the false prophetesses if they thought they could trap others in magic without bringing destruction on themselves. God warned that he was going to tear the wrist charms and veils off individuals that the false prophetesses ensnared. Once freed, these individuals wouldn't again fall prey to magic power. Finally, God told the magician-prophetesses that they would no longer see false visions or practice divination.

Every time I read this incident about the magician-prophetesses, I wonder about their motivation. Were they deliberate charlatans or did they believe their own words and actions? Did they trust what they read in animal entrails or in the way stars aligned? When they went through a ritual to spell a charm, did they then believe that the charm influenced an outcome? Alternatively, were they motivated to get ahead in the world? Did they use magic to provide financially for themselves and children? Whatever the reason for their behavior, the women lied to unsuspecting victims. They conformed to a society where magic was acceptable. They didn't trust God to care for their lives and their future; certainly they didn't discern the will of God for their lives. Ultimately, God condemned their behavior (Romans 12:2).

The Old Testament recorded multiple stories about women's will power, whether or not it was consistent with God's guidelines for righteous behavior. In contrast, New Testament writers recorded fewer incidents of women who wanted something and acted on their desires. One was a woman with a bleeding problem. The woman's story was recorded in all three of the synoptic gospels; however, Mark gave the most detail (Mark 5:25-34). The woman had an issue of blood for twelve years. This description is a polite way of saying that she had her menses continually for twelve years. She spent all of her money going to physicians to get a cure; but physicians weren't able to stop the bleeding. In these ancient times, there was no hormone replacement or hysterectomy (surgical removal of uterus).

The woman didn't just suffer physically, she suffered mentally and spiritually. Jewish Law declared her to be ceremonially unclean due to her bleeding (Leviticus 15:25-27). She couldn't enter the temple for Jewish religious ceremonies. Anything or anyone she touched became unclean, even if she brushed up against another person's clothing in a crowd, such as at a market place.

When the woman heard Jesus was nearby, she thought, "If I just touch his clothes, I will be healed" (Mark 5:28). She braved the crowd, came up behind Jesus, and she touched his cloak. As soon as she touched Jesus, she knew that her bleeding stopped. Probably, she wanted to slip away quietly, but Jesus had another plan. He stopped and asked who touched his clothes. Jesus felt healing power leave him. He wouldn't move forward. Terrified the woman approached

Jesus, fell at his feet, and told him the entire story. Jesus looked at the woman with love, called her "Daughter," and assured her that her faith healed her. Then, Jesus told the woman to go in peace that she was free from her suffering. What a beautiful story of a woman's will power combined with Christ's eagerness to heal a daughter.

Conclusion

A woman's will power came not from an impulse to act, but from acting on an impulse.[1] Bible women's will power was a significant asset in the ancient Near East where men dominated much of society and culture. Often a Bible woman with strong will power needed nothing but herself to change her environment. At times her changes were for the better as in the case of Tamar and sometimes changes were for the worse as with Lot's daughters. For better or for worse, women with strong wills influenced Bible history.

Chapter 4

Influence, Power in Action

In the preceding three chapters, I reviewed personal, positional, and will power. Included were examples of Bible women who used these powers. Chapter 4 zeroes in on Bible women's use of influence. Power is a pre-requisite to influencing others. Bible women weren't much different than women today. They wanted to influence individuals in their environment whether a parent, spouse, tribe, or nation. Bible women used influence to get others to:

- do something or behave in a certain, even different, way
- agree with them, or accept their perspective
- believe what was told to them or accept a recommendation
- think a particular way

Influence is part of every communication and present in almost every human interaction.[5] Influence is power in action. Influence (or persuasion) from other people constantly remakes us, changes us. At times influence is consciously, even purposefully, used to sway another person's opinions or actions. At other times, influence is used unconsciously; yet, the influencer wants an explicit outcome to occur. Influence can produce an effect without apparent exertion of force or giving a direct command. Sometimes influence occurs without a word being spoken. Probably, we have all been influenced by nod (yes) or a shake (no) of the head.

Influence is common; so much a part of the fabric of society, that sometimes it goes unrecognized. Often Bible readers—even women readers—don't recognize when a Bible woman used influence. Yet, these same readers readily identified when a man influenced another man, i.e., a king influenced his soldiers, a priest stirred listeners to action. I believe the gender recognition differences of both women and men were related to expectations for Bible women's behavior. Frequently, when women and men read the Bible today, they aren't expecting to read about influential women; consequently, they don't readily recognize these behaviors in Bible women. In the interest of full disclosure, I want you to know that my enlightened husband remarked to me that Bible women were chattels. This book is one of my efforts to convince him that his perspective of Bible women is incorrect.

Bible women's influence began in the Garden of Eden, extended through Old Testament history, into the New Testament church. Although Bible women's influence often had a different purpose or focus than that of 21st century women, Bible women weren't necessarily less influential. A careful analysis of Bible women's behavior demonstrated that they used the same influence techniques used by women today. They used the same influence techniques used by Bible men.

Researchers identified three categories of positive influence techniques: rational, social, and emotional.[5] Chapter 4 elaborates on these positive influence techniques and gives examples when Bible women used them. Notice I wrote "positive" influence techniques. Not surprisingly, negative influence tactics existed. Bible women weren't above using them to get their way and achieve objectives. In Chapter 4, I discuss negative influence techniques and give examples where Bible women used these techniques.

Rational Influence Techniques

Rational influence techniques include (a) logical persuading, (b) legitimizing, (c) exchanging, and (d) stating.

Logical persuading is the number one influence technique used across the globe. When Bible women used logical persuading to influence others, they used logic, or what passed for logic in their minds, to explain why others should think or act in a certain way. Yet, logical persuading didn't and doesn't work on everyone. A colleague, a philosophy professor, related his attempt to persuade his wife to act in a certain way. He fell back on the, "It's logical" argument. Her comeback was, "Well, logical isn't the only way to think." I wish you could have seen his face when he told me that story. He was incredulous that his beloved wife wouldn't want to think and act logically.

Zelophehad's daughters' appeal to Moses for property rights was an example where Bible women used logical persuasion (Numbers 27:1-11). An earlier Numbers chapter recorded that a census was taken that counted Israelite men twenty years-of-age or older. The census was to be used to allocate land when the Israelites entered the Promised Land. Zelophehad was a man from the tribe of Manasseh who had died in the wilderness. He sired five daughters but no sons; consequently, his daughters wouldn't receive land. Without land the girls would be destitute.

The daughters of Zelophehad went to the Tent of Meeting where Moses and other prominent Israelite men were seated, probably hearing petitions. The five daughters spoke with determination to the assembled leaders: "Our father died in the wilderness. He was not among Korah's followers, who banded together against the Lord, but he died of his own sin and left no sons. Why should our father's name disappear from his clan because he had no son? Give us property among our father's relatives" (Numbers 27:3-4). Moses took the daughters' petition to God. God agreed with Zelophehad's daughters and instituted a new inheritance law for the Israelites. In the Promised Land, the girls would receive a tract of land, thus, increasing their opportunity to receive a marriage offer.

In the New Testament, a woman newly converted to Christianity used logical persuading. Soon after Paul and the other missionaries arrived in Philippi, they went to the river to pray on a Sabbath morning. Lydia, a business woman from Thyatira, was there (Acts 16:11-15). Lydia worshipped God; however, the Bible didn't identify her as a Jew or Gentile. Lydia listened to the missionaries' testimony and accepted Jesus as the Savior of the world and as her Savior. She and her entire household were baptized. Then, Lydia invited the missionaries to stay at her home. Her exact words were, "If you consider me to be a believer in the Lord, come and stay at my house" (Acts 16:15). *The New International Version* (NIV) *Study Bible* recorded that Lydia "persuaded" the missionaries to stay with her, while the Amplified Version (AMP) recorded that Lydia "induced" the missionaries to stay with her.

Legitimizing. Legitimizing is an appeal to authority to influence another. Often appeal to authority resulted in quick compliance; yet, if individuals had no interest or motivation to adhere to authority, legitimizing didn't work on them. Global studies showed that legitimizing was the least effective influence technique.[5] When the Bible was written, the authority of a king or a governor was greater than today. Perhaps, legitimizing was a more important influence technique then than now. Further, many ancient people believed in a god and had a relationship with him or her. Often these ancient people legitimized their behavior by referencing their god's values, commands, and even his/her name.

Job's wife's words demonstrated belief in God when she tried to influence Job to escape his pain (Job 1:13-22). In this Bible story, Satan killed Job's ten children and many of Job's servants. Most of Job's livestock was slaughtered or seized by marauders. Satan struck Job with loathsome sores so that Job was in incessant pain. Unlike Job, Mrs. Job didn't have physical pain to take away her mental grief at the loss of her children. Daily, she witnessed Job's pain and his devolving health. Finally, Mrs. Job told her husband "Renounce God and die" (Job 2:9 AMP). Renounce means to refuse to follow, obey, or recognize any further. When Mrs. Job told Job to renounce God, she showed that she believed that if Job renounced God, God would kill him. Mrs. Job had hit rock bottom in her ability to cope with the loss of her children and her husband's pain. She asked herself how things could get any worse even if God killed Job. If Job was dead, then at least her beloved husband would be pain free.

The widow of a prophet legitimized a request to Elisha by using God's name (2 Kings 4:1-7). Elisha led a band of prophets. One prophet died. His widow went to Elisha and said, "Your servant my husband is dead, and you know he revered the Lord" (2 Kings 4:1). The dead prophet had debts and his creditor planned to take the woman's sons as slaves to pay the debts. The dead prophet's wife didn't ask Elisha for money. She simply told him what was occurring, being sure to legitimize her request with two import facts. First, the woman said that her dead husband was Elisha servant, meaning he was a member of Elisha band of prophets. Second, she avowed that her dead husband revered the Lord who Elisha spoke for in Israel. Elisha asked the woman what she had in her house. The woman replied that she had only a small jar of olive oil. Elisha performed a miracle for the woman by causing the small jar of olive oil to fill so many containers that the woman had enough oil to pay her husband's creditor and live on the money in the future.

In the New Testament, Jesus traveled through Samaria on his way to Galilee (John 4:4-26). He stopped at a town (Sychar) well. His disciples went into town to buy food. While Jesus waited at the well, a Samaritan woman came to draw water. Jesus asked her for a drink. The Samaritan woman was reluctant to give a Jewish man water (or anything else); but, she hid her reluctance behind societal rules in Jewish culture. She expressed shock that a Jewish man would (a) talk to a woman, (b) ask a Samaritan to draw water for him, and (c) ritually contaminate himself by drinking water from a Samaritan's woman's vessel. Jesus responded that if she knew who he was, she would ask him for living water. The Samaritan woman was confused, both by this Jewish man and his words. Still, she thought that having to never thirst again was a good idea. She legitimized her reluctance to ask Jesus for living water with a question in which she referred to a revered ancestor: was Jesus more important than her ancestor Jacob (grandson of Abraham) who dug and used Sychar's well? Certainly, she didn't expect Jesus to respond that indeed he was more important than Jacob. He was the looked-for Messiah.

Negotiating. Negotiating, or exchanging for cooperation, is another rational approach to exerting influence. Negotiating is a *quid quo pro*, you give me x and I will give you y. Negotiating is more effective if the negotiation is understood or implied, rather than stated openly.[5] Bible women sometimes negotiated, or traded, for cooperation. An example is an interaction between Leah and Rachel. These two women were sisters, both married to Jacob (Genesis 30:14-16). Leah's son, Reuben, brought his mother mandrakes. Rachel asked Leah for the mandrakes, but Leah refused to give them to her. Rachel negotiated with Leah to get them. Rachel told Leah that Jacob would sleep with her that night if Leah gave her the mandrakes. Leah accepted Rachel's bargain. Today, most of us don't have a clue why both Bible women valued mandrakes. It was because ancient women believed that mandrakes caused fertility. Rachel who was barren at the time wanted the mandrakes so she would have a baby. Leah wanted them so she would conceive more children.

Another Old Testament story involved Hannah negotiating with God in her prayers (1 Samuel 1:9-27). This incident happened at Shiloh, the center of God worship before the Jerusalem temple was built. Hannah was Elkanah's wife; but, Hannah was unable to conceive children. Hannah wept and prayed before God for children. Bitter at her childless state, Hannah negotiated with God in one of her prayers. She told God that if he gave her a son, she would give the son to the Lord all the days of his life. No razor would ever be used on her son's head. Eventually, Hannah conceived and had a child; his name was Samuel. After Samuel was weaned, Hannah and Elkanah took Samuel to Eli, the chief priest, to live at Shiloh in the Lord's service.

Stating. Stating is asserting what you want or believe. Stating is most effective when influencers are self-confident and state ideas or beliefs in a compelling tone. In the Old Testament, King Lemuel's mother stated how she wanted her son to live and act (Proverbs 31:1-9). She began her statements by twice telling King Lemuel to "Listen."

The Bible recorded her advice as imperative (command) sentences. She told her son:

- don't spend your strength on women
- don't drink wine or crave beer
- don't deprive the oppressed of their rights
- do speak up for those who can't speak for themselves
- do speak up for the rights of the destitute
- do speak up and judge fairly
- do defend the rights of the poor and needy

A problem with stating is that it can cause resistance, particularly if over-used or used in a heavy-handed manner. In the New Testament, a slave girl stated the same message repeatedly. In this story Paul and other missionaries were in Philippi, Greece (Acts 16:16-38). There, they encountered a slave girl who could tell the future because an evil spirit lived inside her. She followed Paul and other missionaries several days, always loudly stating the same words:

"These men are servants of the Most High God, who are telling you the way to be saved" (Acts 16:17). What the girl said was true. Paul and other missionaries were servants of God. They were telling the Philippians how to be saved. The problem was the girl's loud voice and repetitive message harassed the missionaries when they attempted to tell listeners the good news of Christ. Finally, Paul said to the girl's evil spirit, "In the name of Jesus Christ I command you to come out of her" (Acts 16:18). Immediately, the evil spirit left the girl; she was no longer able to foretell. She became quiet and stopped following the missionaries.

Social Influence Techniques

Parallel to four rational influence techniques, there are four social influence strategies.[5] Social strategies depend more on relationships than on logic. Social influence strategies are (a) socializing, (b) appeal to a relationship, (c) consulting, and (d) alliance building

Socializing. When Bible women socialized, they got to know each other through the give and take of conversation. They observed how others behaved in a variety of situations. Like women today, Bible women acted open and friendly as they found common ground with another person. Remember how open and friendly Rebekah acted toward Eliezar when she encountered him at the town spring (Genesis 24:15-27)? Socializing can include complements so others feel good about themselves, which in turn caused them to feel good about the complimenter. After all, if a woman liked something about me, she must be a discerning person. In every culture studied in the 21st century, socializing was used as a strategy to influence others.[5] In some societies, socializing was the best way to influence another person.

Although most Bible women's social contacts were positive or at least benign, Peninnah's contact, or socializing, with Hannah was an exception (1 Samuel 1:1-8). Hannah was the first and much-loved wife of Elkanah, but Hannah was barren. Elkanah married a second woman, Peninnah. Despite Peninnah birthing a number of sons and daughters, Elkanah loved Hannah more than he loved Peninnah. Peninnah was jealous of Elkanah's obvious preference for Hannah. When Peninnah and Hannah were together, Peninnah provoked and irritated Hannah to the point that Hannah wept and wouldn't eat. Nothing Elkanah said consoled Hannah.

An endearing New Testament story that demonstrated socializing in the early church focused on Rhoda (Acts 12:13-16). About ten years after the death of Christ, King Herod Agrippa 1 had the apostle James beheaded and put Peter in prison. The night before Peter's public trial, an angel appeared in Peter's cell. The chains on Peter's hands fell off. The angel led Peter out of the prison, then, left Peter. When Peter realized he was free, he went to Mary's house. Her home was a gathering place for church members. That night church members were there, probably praying for Peter's release.

Mary's house had an outer courtyard door which faced the street. The door was without a window or peep hole. The door was only opened when someone inside the home recognized the knocker's voice. When Peter knocked on the outer door, Rhoda, a servant girl, answered the door. More than likely, she asked, "Who's there?" Rhoda wasn't about to open the door in the middle of the night for just anyone. When Peter identified himself, Rhoda recognized his voice.

In the early church, slaves and/or servants worshiped with owners and free men and women. Rhoda heard Peter preach and pray. Probably, she even had direct conversations with Peter. Rhoda was so excited that Peter was free that she wanted everyone in Mary's house to know. In her joy, Rhoda forgot to open the door and let Peter inside. Instead she ran back to the praying group and told the members that Peter was at the door! Although the church was praying for Peter's release, they told her, "You're out of your mind" (Acts 12:15). Peter kept on knocking at the door and eventually someone opened the door and allowed Peter to join the church members inside.

Appealing to Relationships. At times Bible women attempted to influence a person by appealing to the relationship they had with the person. Two critical points when attempting to influence someone because of a relationship with them are (a) the character or nature of the relationship and (b) at times, the length of the relationship. Bible women in superficial and/or short-term relationships had little or no influence power in the relationship.

In the New Testament, Salome appealed to her relationship with Jesus to request prominence for her two sons (Matthew 20:20). Salome was the mother of James and John and wife of Zebedee. She may have been Jesus' mother's sister. If true, Salome was Jesus' aunt and James and John were Jesus' cousins. Mark documented that Salome traveled with Jesus and her sons from Galilee to Judea (Mark 15:40-41). She helped to fund Jesus' ministry. Salome was at Jesus' crucifixion. She went to Jesus' burial tomb to anoint his body on the first day of the week (Mark 16:1).

Clearly, Salome cared about Jesus. She socialized with him in Galilee and in Judea. Salome believed she knew Jesus well enough and long enough that she could influence him. She approached Jesus and ask him for a "favor" (Matthew 20:20-23). A favor is an act of kindness, or a special privilege or preference. The favor that Salome wanted wasn't for herself, but for her two sons. She wanted Jesus to say that James and John would sit on his right and left hand in his kingdom. Jesus refused Salome's request saying that he didn't have the power to grant it. God would decide who sat at Jesus' right and left hands in heaven. Although Jesus refused Salome's request, she continued to follow and support him.

Consulting. Consulting is co-opting others to define and solve a problem. When Bible women used consulting, they engaged listeners and influenced them by asking questions. Consulting works well in almost all societies. A challenge with consulting is whether or not targeted individual cared about the issue, or if it impacted their lives. If not, the influence target (influencee) wouldn't participate, or participated only minimally, to define or solve the problem.

A Shunammite woman used consulting to get the prophet Elisha to help her. The spectrum of events and resulting emotions seen in the Shunammite woman's life was incredible (2 Kings 4:8-37). When we first met her, she was accepting, even reconciled to her motherless state. Her husband was old. They had no children. Because Elisha appreciated that the Shunammite woman gave him a furnished room, Elisha brought about a miracle—the Shunammite woman became pregnant and gave birth to a son. One morning he went with his father to the fields. There, the son developed an excruciating headache. The reapers took him to his mother in the house. Then, a mother's worst nightmare occurred. Her son died. Sobbing inwardly, the woman proceeded calmly. She took the boy's body to Elisha's room and placed him on Elisha's bed. She left the room, firmly closing the door.

The woman secured a donkey and servant from her husband and rode the approximate twenty-five miles to Elisha's home. Probably, she prayed the entire way that the prophet would be there and that he would assist her. The Shunammite woman arrived at Elisha's home, caught hold of Elisha's feet, and said, "Did I ask you for a son? Didn't I tell you, 'Don't raise my hopes?'" (2 Kings 4:28). The Shunammite woman couldn't get the words that her son was dead past her lips; however, Elisha surmised that the son was very ill or dead and the Shunammite woman came to influence him to return the boy to life. The Shunammite woman insisted she would only go home if Elisha accompanied her. At the woman's home Elisha found the woman's dead son. After praying, Elisha restored the boy's life.

In the New Testament an example of a woman involved in consultation occurred after Paul was arrested and confined for two years by the Roman Governor Felix. When Governor Felix was replaced with Festus, King Agrippa and his sister Bernice came to visit Governor Festus. Festus asked King Agrippa to hear Paul's case and help him make a decision on how to handle it (Acts chapter 27). After hearing Paul's defense against the Jew's accusations, the Governor, King Agrippa, and Bernice left the room "talking with one another" (Acts 30-31). Bernice was a canny advisor to King Agrippa. She was involved actively in the final decision to send Paul to Rome for Caesar to decide Paul's case.

Alliance building. The final social approach that Bible women used to influence others was alliance building. Alliance building moved beyond an individual being the influencer. The influencer used other individuals, or groups, to gain cooperation from the target of the influence.[5] Alliance building is problematic because individuals change their minds.

In the Bible a simple example of alliance building was Naaman being healed of leprosy (2 Kings 5:1-6). Naaman was the army commander of Aram. The king of Aram regarded Naaman highly because through Naaman the Lord gave Aram many victories. During one raid into Israel, Naaman took a young Israelite girl captive. The Israelite girl impressed Naaman. He gave her to his wife for a slave. The Israelite girl cared about both Naaman and his wife.

One day the captive Israelite girl told her mistress that if Naaman went to the prophet in Samaria, the prophet would cure Naaman's skin disease. The girl didn't try to influence Naaman directly; instead she built an alliance with her mistress. The young Israelite captive accepted that her mistress would have a better chance than she to influence Naaman. Naaman's wife told her husband the girl's words. Naaman told the King of Aram. The King of Aram encouraged Naaman to go to Israel. He sent a letter with Naaman to Israel's king, "With this letter I am sending with my servant Naaman so that you may cure him of his leprosy" (2 Kings 5:6). The slave girl built an alliance with her mistress to influence Naaman to visit Elisha. The King of Aram attempted to build an alliance with the King of Israel to get Israel's king involved in Naaman's cure.

In the New Testament, Martha attempted to build an alliance with Jesus. When Jesus visited Bethany, Martha opened her home to him. Martha loved Jesus and began to prepare a sumptuous meal for him and his disciples. Instead of helping Martha prepare the meal, her younger sister Mary sat at Jesus' feet listening to his teaching. Martha became distracted by all the needed preparation and perhaps a little resentful that Mary got to hear Jesus while she was left with all the work. Martha said to Jesus, "Lord, don't you care that my sister has left me to do the work myself? Tell her to help me!" (Luke 11:40). Martha wanted Jesus to tell Mary to get up and assist her with meal preparation. Jesus refused to buy into Martha's attempted to build an alliance with him. His response to Martha was that Mary chose the better activity, that is, she chose to listen to his teachings rather than prepare a meal. Because Mary chose the better activity, he wouldn't tell her to help with meal preparation.

Emotional Influence Techniques

In addition to four rational and four social techniques to influence others, two emotional approaches were recognized: (a) appealing to values and (b) modeling.[5] Emotional influencers are powerful. When a Bible woman made an emotional appeal, she targeted the heart of the listener.

<u>Appealing to values</u>. Appealing to values was the opposite of logical persuasion.[5] Appealing to values was and is the best influence technique for building commitment. Today, appealing to values is used by spiritual leaders, fundraisers, politicians, and even business leaders, when they focus on company values. When God told Jacob to return to Canaan, Jacob sent word to his two wives (Leah and Rachel) to come into the fields where he was caring for his flocks (Genesis 31:1-18). Jacob told his wives that God directed him to return to Canaan. Jacob wanted to know what the two of them thought. Jacob outlined problems of staying with his wives' father and his brothers-in-law.

In just about all Bible stories which included both Leah and Rachel, the two of them were in conflict; but, in this story, they stood together. Why? Because the issue was about ancient Near East values! Jacob's wives declared that their father sold them to Jacob and spent the money paid for them. According to Mesopotamian law, the money or property a son-in-law gave to the bride's father at the time he married a daughter was to be retained. The money was to be available for the daughter should she later need it, as for example, if her husband died without siring a son to care for the mother in her later years. Sometimes the bride money was given to the couple's children. Laban didn't keep money equivalent to seven years of Jacob's work for either of his daughters. Laban spent the money.

In the first century, Peter traveled throughout the country encouraging the new churches. At Joppa a widow, Tabitha (Dorcas), became sick and died. Hearing that Peter was in a nearby town, Joppa disciples sent for him. When Peter arrived in Joppa, he was taken to the room where Tabitha's body lay. Many widows stood weeping around the bod. They showed Peter the many robes and other clothing that Tabitha made for others. There was no record that the weeping women asked Peter to bring Tabitha back to life. Their sorrow in combination with the good deeds done by Tabitha influenced Peter to pray for the restoration of Tabitha's life. Appealing to values was most powerful when the message was aligned with the target's (Peter) beliefs.[5] The weeping women wanted Peter to pray for Tabitha's restored life. Their desire was consistent with Peter's beliefs about the value of good deeds in the new church.

Role modeling. Behaving in ways Bible women wanted others to behave was an emotional influence tactic. Today this approach is called role modeling, teaching, coaching, counseling, or mentoring. In Bible times, parents, priests, and public figures influenced others through modeling. For Bible women the effectiveness of role modeling as an influence technique was problematic because often Bible women modeled behaviors they didn't want others to follow.

The Bible story of Rizpah demonstrated positive role modeling (2 Samuel 21:1-10). By her consistent, caring behavior toward her sons' dead bodies, Rizpah influenced King David without uttering a word. During David's reign, Israel experienced a three-year famine because no rain fell on the land. God told David that the famine was the result of Saul killing and almost decimating the Gibeonites, a non-Israelite clan who signed a peace treaty with Israel 400 years earlier. David asked the remaining Gibeonites what amends he could make so that they would lift their curse from Israel. The Gibeonites demanded seven of King Saul's descendants to kill. David turned over five sons of Saul's daughter, Merab, and the two sons of Saul's concubine, Rizpah. The Gibeonites murdered and exposed the bodies at Gibeah, the home town of both the Gibeonites and of King Saul's ancestors.

Rizpah was in a terrible position (2 Samuel 21:11-14). Her father Aiah was likely dead. Her husband, King Saul, was dead. Now, her sons were dead. What was she to do? Who would provide for her? Rizpah's next action surprised all who noted it. She took sackcloth, spread it out on a rock near her sons' bodies, and sat on the cloth. By day Rizpah kept birds off her sons' bodies and by night she fought wild animals to keep them away. The odor of her sons' decaying bodies was painful. Rizpah remained at the site of the exposed bodies for at least six-to-eight months, to include during the heat of a long Israel summer.

When David learned of Rizpah's action, he gathered the bones of the seven men murdered at Gibeah and buried them along with the bones of King Saul and Jonathan in Saul's father's tomb at Zela, Benjamin. Both Rizpah and her sons were pawns in this Bible story, but Rizpah's action is one of the Bible's greatest stories of a woman role model.

In the New Testament, Philip's daughters were role models in the early Christian church. This Philip was one of the seven Jewish men chosen by the Jerusalem church to minister to Greek widows. During the persecution of the Jerusalem church, Philip moved Caesarea. His four daughters were unmarried. Each daughter had the gift of prophecy. Paul cited prophecy as the most desirable spiritual gift (1 Corinthians 14:1) and listed prophets before teachers in ministry gifts (1 Corinthians 12:28). In addition to being roles models of prophetesses in the early Christian church, the four women were role models of care for an aging father in his home.

Negative Influence Tactics

Bible women used, and individual's today use, four negative influence tactics: (a) avoiding, (b) manipulating, (c) intimidating, and (d) threatening. These influence techniques were negative because they took away the other person's legitimate right to say "No." They forced individuals to comply with something contrary to their wishes, best interests, and/or mislead them. Sometimes negative techniques forced others to act when they would rather not act.

Avoidance. Avoidance is the most commonly used dark-side tactic. Avoidance occurred when an individual refused to take responsibility; thus, they avoided a conflict. Avoidance forced another individual to act. Frequently, avoidance occurred, and still occurs, in cultures where preserving harmony was more important than taking action.

After Prince Amnon raped Princess Tamar, a virgin, she didn't return to the palace and demand that her father, King David, secure justice for her (2 Samuel chapter 13). Princess Tamar could have reminded her father that she only went to Prince Amnon's house because King David ordered her to do so. Instead, Tamar went to her brother's, Absalom, home. Tamar kept silent and avoided a conflict with her father, King David. By her actions Tamar influenced her brother, Prince Absalom, to secure justice for her. Two years later Absalom killed Prince Amnon in retaliation for raping Tamar. Princess Tamar's choice to avoid a conflict with her father, ultimately led to a civil war in Israel.

Manipulation. Manipulation is disguising intentions or intentionally withholding information another person needs to make the right decision.[5] Manipulation includes lies, deceit, hoaxes, swindles, and cons. Rachel manipulated her father, Laban. Seven days after Jacob and his family left Laban's home in Paddan Aram, Laban caught up with Jacob. Laban asked Jacob why Jacob stole his household gods. Jacob was flabbergasted by the accusation. Jacob told Laban if anyone in Jacob's household had Laban's household gods, the person wouldn't live. Household gods were usually small images made from metal or wood that represented gods worshipped by the family. Unknown to Jacob, his wife, Rachel, stole her father's gods.

Jacob gave Laban permission to enter each tent and search for the images. When Laban entered Rachel's tent, Rachel remained seated on a camel saddle while her father searched the tent. Rachel begged her father not to be angry. The reason she didn't rise was because she had her menses. In reality, Rachel hid Laban's household gods in her camel's saddle. By not getting up from the saddle, Rachel prevented Laban from searching in or under it. Rachel's action deceived both her father and her husband.

Intimidation. Intimidation is the preferred tactic of bullies. When bullies deliberately intimidated other persons, they imposed themselves or their ideas on others. Often bullies intruded or force themselves into an individual's personal space. Intimidating individuals can be loud, overbearing, abrasive, and insensitive. A brief prayer by Nehemiah, a restoration governor over Judea, showed he was intimidated by the prophetess Noadiah who lived in Jerusalem at the time. Nehemiah prayed that God would remember Noadiah and other prophets who tried to make him afraid, or intimidate him (Nehemiah 6:14). Because Nehemiah named Noadiah in his prayer, possibly she was the head of a group of prophets that opposed Nehemiah's actions. Bible readers aren't certain what Noadiah did that intimidated Nehemiah; but, by his own admission the prophetess Noadiah intimidated this strong leader.

In the New Testament Jesus told a short parable that involved a persistent widow and a corrupt judge (Luke 18:1-8). The widow kept appearing before the judge with the same plea. She demanded justice against her adversary. The widow appeared before the judge so often that he felt intimidated by her persistence. Finally, the judge decided to grant the woman justice so she would stop haranguing him. The Bible didn't record that the widow was loud or overbearing; just that her persistence intimidated the corrupt judge.

Threat. Tyrants, dictators, and despots threaten friends and foes alike to get compliance. A threat expressed intention to inflict damage or injury, or do something evil. Generally, the threat was: do what I wish or I will punish you and/or those you love. If tyrants used and followed up on threats enough times, they simply give an order and subjects obeyed. The tyrants, "or I will" was no longer necessary. Listeners knew a threat was present. Often people who were threatened felt insecure or anxious, sometimes they were angry. Rachel, Jacob's much-loved wife, made a threat. She told Jacob, "Give me children, or I shall die!" (Genesis 30:1). Jacob was threatened by Rachel's outburst. He didn't want to lose his beloved Rachel. At the same time, Jacob was angry. He had no power to change the situation. Jacob pushed back at Rachel, angrily saying that he wasn't God to ensure that she had children.

Conclusion

Despite using power to influence individuals, Bible women weren't always able to do so. Some times their influence failed for legitimate reasons such as the influence target had goals and values different from those of the Bible woman. At other times, Bible women attempted to influence others on only one occasion. When that attempt failed, they gave up. Have you ever wondered how many times Rachel approached her servant Bilhah and Jacob before they agreed to have intercourse and conceive a baby for her? Likely, it was more than one time; further, Rachel likely used a number of influence strategies, some positive and some negative.

Bible women learned and used influence techniques acceptable in their culture. At times, the woman's influence was ethical and done with integrity. In these instances, targets (influencees) chose to be persuaded, that is, to act in a certain way. Influence targets had complete knowledge before they complied or committed to an action. At other times, Bible women used avoidance, manipulation, intimidation, or threat to influence others.

Generally, individuals respond to the same influence techniques that they use. A maxim in social psychology is that subordinates know more about superiors than superiors know about subordinates. Reason for this almost universal phenomenon is that subordinates study or spend more time observing supervisors (to learn how they act) than supervisors spend studying subordinates. In the ancient Near East, society was largely patriarchal. Bible women observed men in their environment. They knew which influence tactics men, i.e., the father, husband, king, used. In turn, they used these same influence tactics to achieve their objectives when they dealt with men.

10 Bible Women who used Power and Influence

A superficial read of the Bible leaves the impression that women had secondary roles in ancient Near East society and culture. A deeper look showed that they were anything but subservient. Bible women were strong, powerful, and influential. They may not have carried a brief case, had their nails professionally manicured, or participated in power lunches; but, they influenced, perhaps at times even managed, their worlds.

Section 2 contains individual chapters on ten women who I considered the most powerful and influential throughout Bible history. When analyzing the life of each woman, I pointed out where and how each used both personal and positional power; and when a Bible woman's primary strength was the power of her will. These women were far from perfect. They used negative as well as positive influence tactics to get what they wanted.

Descriptions—appearance, words, motives, and thoughts—of early Bible women were often more complete than description of women who lived in later Bible chronology. As the Bible unfolded, space allocated to women lessened to the point where the prophets had almost nothing to say about them. New Testament writers provided only brief anecdotes about women. Yet, if there is one insight we learn from reading the Bible, the amount of copy (number of verses) doesn't mean much. For example, Mary, Christ's mother, had proportionally few verses allocated to her than allocated to Sarah or Ruth. Yet, no Bible woman was more important than Mary.

Chapter 5

Eve, Not Second Best

Genesis chapters 1-4

Who better than Eve to begin a book about the influence of Bible women? Eve's influence echoes through millennia to our 21st century world. Both Adam and Eve were created by God, however, God created them at different times. God created Adam first. Adam had a host of experiences before Eve arrived on the scene. God gave Adam a home in a beautiful garden, the Garden of Eden. In the Hebrew language, Eden means "delight."[6] Naturally, Adam explored his delightful home.

Adam noticed that his garden contained different types of plants. In the center were two special trees: the Tree of Life and the Tree of the Knowledge of Good and Evil. The latter tree produced fruit, but God told Adam that he couldn't eat it. If Adam ate fruit from this tree, he would die. Although Adam never saw anything die, God made sure that Adam understood what death meant—Adam's body would cease to function, to breathe, to think, and to be. God assigned Adam work. Adam tended the plants and protected his garden-home. God brought animals and birds for Adam to name. It is hard to know how long this naming process took; however, at the end of it, Adam realized that none of the animals were a suitable mate for him. Adam felt lonely even though he was surrounded by a myriad of plants and animals and had God to talk with.

God concluded that it wasn't good for Adam to be alone. Adam needed a mate just like the animals had a mate. God created a wife for Adam; her name was Eve. She, too, was made in the image of God. Now, Adam had a suitable companion and someone to share life. Eve alleviated Adam's loneliness. Adam was excited to have Eve in his world. Just as Adam wanted to tend and protect his garden home, Adam wanted to tend and protect Eve, that beautiful companion that God gave him.

In the delightful garden, God spent time with Adam. After God created Eve, God spent time with both Adam and Eve. Because Adam and God had time together and experiences before God created Eve, Eve may have felt a little left out. I can imagine Adam saying to Eve, "God told me that I couldn't eat from the Tree of Knowledge of Good and Evil." Maybe God reminded Adam: "Remember, you named that animal a badger?" Or God said something like, "Remember when I told you........." Perhaps I am projecting my 21st century feelings onto Eve; however, being a woman who came into the God-Adam relationship after it was established, I would have noticed the comradery between the two of them. I would have felt a little left out, even a little diminished or inferior. They seemed to know so much more than I did.

My husband, Bruce, is a wonderful, spiritual man; he reminds me of Adam. We've been married over 25 years. Bruce is from northern Idaho and was reared in an area of hard rock miners. Bruce believes that he needs to take care of me. Sometimes I like his caretaking. Really, I have no desire to pump my own gasoline or wash my own car. But, sometimes, I feel smothered by his directions for my life. I wonder if Eve felt this way. Did she ever want to say to Adam, "Hey, I can figure that out for myself?" The reason I don't get annoyed at Bruce is twofold. First, I know his motivation is love for me. Second, I love him and never want to hurt his feelings. Each time I read the story of Adam and Eve, I hope that Eve understood that she had power over Adam and could influence him because he loved her.

One day Adam and Ever were near the center of the garden. They could see the Tree of Knowledge of Good and Evil. That day trouble entered Adam and Eve's paradise in the form of a snake. Although Genesis didn't specifically say so, Christians believe that Satan was in the snake. The snake started a conversation by asking if God really said that they "must not eat from any tree in the garden?" Eve, not Adam, corrected the snake. She said that they could eat from all trees, except one. Eve told the serpent that she and Adam couldn't even touch the Tree of Knowledge of Good and Evil or they would die. Does it sound to you as if the snake/Satan wanted to socialize with Adam and Eve? Perhaps even way back in Eden, Satan knew that people find it harder to say "No' to someone they know than someone they don't know.

Eve's response to the snake was noteworthy. Remember, she wasn't with Adam when God told him not to eat from the Tree of

Knowledge of Good and Evil. Possibly, in his zeal to protect his helpmate, Adam exaggerated God's admonishment. That is, Adam told Eve that they couldn't even touch the Tree of Knowledge of Good and Evil. Alternatively, Eve herself may have exaggerated Adam's instructions. On her own, Eve conjectured that neither Adam nor she could touch the Tree.

The serpent addressed his rebuttal to Eve. Possibly, Satan observed that as early as the Garden of Eden the woman selected and gathered food which she and Adam ate. The serpent said that Adam and Eve wouldn't die if they ate from the Tree of Knowledge of Good and Evil. Rather, the two of them would be like God himself, knowing what was right and wrong.

According to Jewish legend, the serpent pushed Eve against the Tree of Knowledge of Good and Evil.[7] Eve didn't die when she touched the tree. Immediately, the snake said, "See, touching the Tree doesn't cause death." The snake's action and Eve being alive, caused Eve to doubt that the Tree of Knowledge of Good and Evil was harmful. Then, the snake shook the Tree violently and fruit fell to the ground. The snake ate some of the fruit and didn't die. Eve further doubted if the Tree's fruit was deadly.

The Bible recorded that Eve saw that the fruit of the Tree of Knowledge of Good and Evil was attractive and good for food. And, if legend can be believed, the tree and its fruit didn't cause death when they were touched.[7] Notice the role of influence in this situation. The snake influenced Eve by showing her that she didn't die when she touched the Tree of Knowledge of Good and Evil. Further, the snake didn't die when it ate the fruit. The snake "role modeled" that death didn't occur when the forbidden fruit was eaten. Further, the snake averred (stated) that Eve would become like God knowing right from wrong if she ate from the Tree of Knowledge of Good and Evil.

I'm going to take a short digression at this point in Eve's story, perhaps because I am somewhat critical of Eve's behavior. Those of us who are members of the Judeo-Christian faith "know" Eve shouldn't have eaten fruit from the Tree of Knowledge of Good and Evil. Just the name of the Tree says it all, i.e., evil; yet, to Eve the Tree didn't have a pejorative name. Possibly, it didn't even have a special name. It was just a tree that God planted which grew in the middle of the Garden of Eden. Eve wasn't socialized in childhood Sunday school to know the outcome of her actions. We know the fallout from Eve's actions. She was without that knowledge.

Eve wanted to know more than she did. She wanted to know things just like God knew things. Possibly, Eve didn't want to rely on God or Adam telling her what to think or do. She wanted to make up her mind about events including what was good and evil. When Eve opted to eat fruit from the Tree of Knowledge of Good and Evil, she sinned by disobeying God. At the same time, Eve was gullible. The New Testament described Eve as being deceived (1 Timothy 2:14).

In one of my first jobs, my supervisor told me that I was "gullible;" she wasn't giving me a compliment. As I look back on her assessment, I realize she was correct. I was gullible. My only defense was that in my world view, people were truthful and/or saw the world as I did. Since then I learned that individuals do lie, even when a lie has no advantage. Also, different world views result in individuals interpreting the same event differently. I believe that Eve was gullible because she had no experience with anyone or anything misrepresenting the truth to her.

Satan told Eve a lie and that lie had a purpose. Satan wanted Eve to disobey God. Eve ate the fruit and didn't immediately die. Possibly, Eve thought, "Okay, maybe the snake is right." Then, Eve gave some fruit to Adam who was with her. Adam ate the fruit. Notice the influence that Eve had over Adam. According to the Bible, Eve didn't say anything to Adam. Instead, Eve "modeled" what she wanted Adam to do, i.e., eat the fruit. To Adam Eve's influence, exhibited by her actions (role modeling), was more important than God's prohibition.

From the beginning of time, a woman was able to sway her husband's behavior, perhaps even against his better judgement. A long time ago, I heard a minister say that Adam loved Eve so much that he didn't want to live without her; thus, he was willing to eat the forbidden fruit along with her. If his mate died, Adam wanted to die.

Every Sunday school child knows what happened next. Adam and Eve became aware that they were naked. They made fig leaf clothes to cover themselves. When God confronted Adam with their disobedience, Adam blamed Eve, and Eve blamed the serpent. The ultimate judge, God held all three accountable for their disobedience. God demonstrated that sin had consequences. In this case, Adam and Eve were expelled from their garden paradise and not allowed to re-enter.

Now we come to page two so-to-speak of the story: Adam and Eve after Eden. The Bible doesn't say where they lived. Possibly, it was in a cave or Adam built a hut out of plants and/or animal skins. He tilled the land for food and kept livestock for milk and skins to keep the family warm in colder months. As Adam attempted to secure a safe home and acquire food for his family, he felt his work was never done. How could Adam not resent Eve for loss of Eden? In Eden, caring for plants was a joy. Outside of Eden, planting and harvesting crops and caring for livestock were work!

Eve foraged for food and attempted to grow garden plants similar to those in Eden. She prepared meals for herself and Adam, and later for the children. Maybe, Eve blamed Adam for the loss of Eden. Adam should have more accurately told her what God said about the Tree of Knowledge of Good and Evil. If she knew the full truth, she wouldn't have been deceived by the serpent. Why didn't Adam stop her from taking the forbidden fruit? He was there with her. Importantly, Eve may have felt hurt each time she remembered that when God asked Adam what occurred, Adam blamed her.

Part of God's consequences of Eve's sin was that she desired Adam sexually. As a result, Eve became pregnant. Eve gave birth not in the pain-free bliss of Eden, but in the hostile environment outside the garden. Her first son was a boy who Eve named Cain. Cain means "with the help of the Lord I have brought forth a man" (Genesis 4:1). Eve's name for her first-born son acknowledged that her labor was painful and childbirth difficult. She only got through them with the help of God. Yet, Eve was excited about having a male child. Would Cain be the one to crush Satan's head and restore her and Adam to Eden?

As her first son and with the possibility of Eden restored, Eve doted on Cain. Just as any mother delighted to see her child speak his first words or take his first steps, Eve delighted to see Cain grow.

Because Eve and Adam were created as adults, Cain was their first experience with a child's growth and development. Probably, Eve breast fed Cain until her breasts no longer produced milk. Eve's indulgent focus on Cain influenced Cain to believe he was "special." Adam loved Eve and wanted Eve to be happy; consequently, Adam may have been lenient with Cain. Adam didn't give Cain the discipline he deserved.

Several years later Eve birthed a second son, Abel. The name Abel came from *hebel*, which in Hebrew meant "breath or what passes away without leaving anything significant" (Genesis 4:2) This name sounds like Eve gained some awareness that human life could be short. Possibly, she gave birth to another child that died at birth or shortly afterward. Certainly by this time, Eve saw animals die.

Cain and Abel grew into adult hood. Their vocations mirrored Adam's ways of providing for the family. Cain was a farmer and Abel a herdsman. Both sons learned from Adam that they needed to make sacrifices to God for all the good gifts God gave them, i.e., fruit from trees, increase in size of flocks, farm produce. Abel's sacrifice was the choice animals from his flock. Cain offered God some, but not his best crops. God accepted Abel's sacrifice because Abel gave the best he had. God didn't accept Cain's sacrifice because he didn't give his best crops to God.

Have you ever wondered where Cain's best crops went? Would Cain have taken them to his mother who doted on him? Because of Eve and Cain's close relationship, Cain may have wanted his best for Eve. Very likely, Eve never told Cain to bring his best produce to her; but Eve praised Cain when he offered her succulent, beautiful produce. Eve's influence on Cain was emotional, she appealed to his heart. Further, Cain, like Eve, may have wanted recognition for what he contributed. That recognition most often came from his mother.

Cain was jealous that God accepted Abel's sacrifice. Likely, God also accepted Adam's sacrifice. Cain's sacrifice was the only one God didn't accept. Over time, Cain brooded. His jealousy of Abel escalated. Finally, in a fit of anger, Cain killed Abel. The Bible was silent on the ages of the two sons when the murder occurred. The Bible wasn't silent on Cain's response when God asked him where

Abel was. Petulantly, Cain answered, "Am I my brother's keeper?" denying that he knew Abel's whereabouts (Genesis 4:9).

When Cain killed Abel, Eve lost both her first-born and second-born son. Abel was dead and Cain exiled from the family's home. Eve was devastated. According to Jewish legend, Adam and Eve didn't live together for a time after Abel's death.[7] The legend can't be verified; however, Eve may have stopped being intimate with Adam for a time. Severe loss can lead to depression, which can cause lack of sexual intimacy in a marriage.

When Adam lived 130 years, Eve birthed a son who she named Seth. With Seth's birth, Eve said that God gave her another offspring in place of Abel who Cain killed. The Genesis recorder wrote that Seth was in Adam's likeness and image. When Eve birthed Cain and Abel, neither son was described as in Adam's likeness or image (Genesis 5:3); however, the Genesis 5:3 verse doesn't mean that Adam wasn't the father of Eve's first two sons. "In the image of" meant that Seth was more like Adam. Adam made sure that Seth was reared with Godly values rather than with his mother's indulgent influence.

After Seth's birth the Bible gives no additional information about Eve. Adam lived 930 years; however, Eve's life span wasn't specified. Eve could have died significantly earlier than Adam, perhaps in childbirth or by accident or disease. The Bible gave no information that Adam took a second wife. The marriage of Adam and Eve was monogamous.

Conclusion

The mother of the human race was an intelligent, thinking woman who didn't want to be told what to do, even when the teller was her Creator-God. Genesis showed only brief snapshots of Eve's behavior; yet, the snapshots depicted a woman who knew she was co-equal with men in her life. Eve wanted power over her own life and at times over the lives of her husband and sons. Her power sources were attraction, role, and relationship (history) with the men in her life.

Because Eve was physically weaker than Adam, and her sons, Eve couldn't physically compel them to act the way she wanted them to act. Eve discovered early that she could use influence to gain what she wanted. Common influence techniques Eve used were referencing a legitimate authority, that is, God; stating something as fact in a knowledgeable, firm manner; and role modeling what she wanted done. Very likely, Eve used negative influence tactics, that is, manipulation, in some interactions with Adam and with Cain.

Unfortunately for Eve and for mankind, Eve's power and influence didn't always lead to optimal outcomes. Eve learned that sometimes influence had negative, or unintended, consequences. Eve learned, or could have learned, a lot about power and influence inside and outside of Eden. In the 21st century, women ponder Eve's decisions and behavior. Most of us wouldn't want to be Eve. The learning curve for her use of power and influence was way too steep.

Chapter 6

Sarah, Relationship Power in Action

Genesis chapter 12-23

Three women were prominent in Abram's life: Sarai, Hagar, and Keturah. Each gave him one or more sons. By far the most influential was Sarai. After Eve, Sarai was the first woman profiled in the Bible. Sarai was Abram's wife and half-sister. Abram and Sarai had the same father, but not the same mother. A marriage between a man and woman this closely related was acceptable in the ancient Near East.

The Bible recorded how Sarai's life unfolded from about age 65 until her death at 127 years. Yet, the Bible provided no information on when she married Abram or if she loved him. We are told that she was 10 years younger than Abram. In the ancient Near East, girls were wed soon after they started menstruating, so possibly Sarai married Abram when she was 12-15 years-of-age. Abram would have been 22-25 years-old. Sarai was barren, the couple had no children.

To appreciate Sarai's influence and power, I investigated her life concurrent with Abram's journey in response to God's direction and to find pastures for his flocks. As you read through this chapter, you will see that Sarai had two main sources of power in relation to Abram. They were history (relationship) and attraction power. Sarai was Abram's wife for over 100 years and she was beautiful.

God first spoke to Abram in Haran and told him to go to Canaan. At the time Abram worshiped Chaldean gods. Can you imagine Abram going to Sarai and saying that a new and different God spoke to him? This God wanted Abram and Sarai to leave Haran and travel to Canaan. Further, if Abram followed this new God's direction, God promised that he would: (a) make Abram into a great nation, (b) bless Abram, (c) make Abram's name great, and (d) bless those who blessed Abram and curse those who cursed Abram. God said that through Abram all the nations of the earth would be blessed.

Probably, Abram secured Sarai's buy-in the moment he repeated God's promise to make Abram a great nation. A great nation meant that Abram would sire offspring. By this time Sarai and Abram had been married around 50 years. Even though Sarai was barren, in those years Abram didn't take a second wife. Hearing that Abram would become the father of a great nation meant Sarai would be its mother. She was Abram's only wife. At last, Sarai had hope of conceiving a child. Sarai added every rational, social, and emotional influence technique in her arsenal to support Abram making the journey to Canaan. When Abram was 75 and Sarai 65 years old, they left Haran for Canaan.

Abram was a herdsman. His wealth was his flocks of sheep and goats; however, Abram owned other livestock, i.e., camels, cattle, and donkeys. The trip from Haran to Canaan (around 600 miles) was slow to allow animals to graze along the way. Sarai walked and/or rode on an animal. Either way, her days were long. She was jarred with each step the animal took. At day's end, her back hurt; her legs were numb. Yet, Sarai didn't complain. At no point did Sarai try to influence Abram to stop traveling and build a home at a good location between Haran and Canaan. Daily, Sarai got off her animal, set up a tent, and prepared a meal for Abram. Her eyes were set on Canaan. When the family arrived in Canaan, God appeared to Abram again and told him "To your offspring I will give this land" (Genesis 12:7). When Abram told Sarai God's words, she became even more hopeful that she would be a mother.

Several years later a severe famine occurred in Canaan. Abram moved his family and flocks to Egypt. Before entering Egypt, Abram instructed Sarai to tell Egyptians that she was his sister, rather than his wife. Abram reasoned that Sarai was beautiful; consequently, the Egyptians would kill him in order to acquire Sarai. I wonder if Abram said, "If you love me, Sarai, you will go along with this plan to protect me" as part of his directions to Sarai.

The Bible gave no indication that Sarai attempted to influence Abram to acknowledge her as his wife when they entered Egypt. She obeyed her husband. Subsequent events evolved exactly as Abram predicted. Egyptian officials praised Sarai's beauty to pharaoh. Pharaoh ordered Sarai to be brought to his palace. Sarai became pharaoh's wife which meant that he had sexual intercourse with her.

Pharaoh treated Abram well for Sarai's sake. Abram acquired sheep, cattle, donkeys, and camels as well as male and female servants. Despite Abram prospering in Egypt, God wasn't happy with the situation. God inflicted a serious disease on pharaoh and his household. Pharaoh found out that the reason for the disease was that Sarai was Abram's wife. Pharaoh confronted Abram with his duplicity, returned Sarai to Abram, and expelled them from Egypt. Pharaoh gave Sarai a personal slave, Hagar, when Sarai left pharaoh's harem.

How distasteful! The godly Abram gave his wife Sarai to pharaoh to protect his own skin. What did Sarai think about her husband's actions? Was she just a "thing" or commodity for Abram to use as needed? At the least, Sarai was hurt and possibly embarrassed in front of camp servants. Her hurt may have shifted into resentment and bitterness toward Abram and toward his God. At the same time, Sarai knew she was culpable in this horrendous situation. She didn't protest when Abram told her his strategy for protecting his life in Egypt. She didn't volunteer to the Egyptians that she was Abram's wife.

After their stay in Egypt, Abram and Sarai returned to Canaan. Again, God promised Abram that all the land he could see would belong to his offspring. Despite this seemingly good news from God, this could have been the point where Sarai started to have doubts. Although God promised that Abram's offspring would be numerous, not once did God say that Sarai would be their mother. Sarai pondered God's exact words to Abram. She put them together with Abram's action in Egypt. Sarai began to doubt that she was as important to God's plan and to her husband as she originally thought.

Years passed and still Abram and Sarai had no children. Then, God appeared to Abram a fourth time. God affirmed that a son of Abram's flesh and blood would be his heir. Sarai noted that again she wasn't named in God's promise. Sarai felt discouraged and inadequate. She was a wife—the only wife—of a rich man; but, she couldn't give him children. Sarai may have concluded that Abram's marriage and sexual loyalty to her kept him from fathering a son.

Clearly, Abram wasn't going to do anything to get an heir. She had to take action. Determinedly, Sarai came up with a plan. After Sarai decided what to do, she used the full weight of her position as Abram's wife of about 70 years (role and relationship power). Sarai decided to follow Chaldean custom and build a family through her servant. In ancient Near East cultures, it was acceptable for a barren wife to assign a slave or servant to have intercourse with the wife's husband. Children from the union of husband and slave belonged to the wife. The wife had full authority over the children to include the right to name them.

How did Sarai influence Abram to father a son with her slave Hagar? First, Sarai told Abram that God prevented her from having children. Ancient Near East peoples believed that human fertility was controlled by a deity. By making her sterility God's decision, Sarai legitimized her proposal to Abram. Second, Sarai directed (stated) Abram to have intercourse with Hagar, her maid. Most likely Sarai's statements were compelling because she believed what she said was right. Finally, her decisions and actions were within the parameters of Chaldean values.

Some Bible commentators suggested that Sarai had too much influence on Abram. Yet, some of Sarai's influence on Abram may have been because he wanted exactly what Sarai proposed, that is, Abram wanted a son desperately. Alternatively, Abraham allowed himself to be influenced by Sarai because he felt guilty for the way he treated her in Egypt.

Sarai's choice of Hagar for the mother of her son is perplexing. Hagar was an Egyptian, not a Chaldean. Why didn't Sarai choose a woman of her own culture? Perhaps, Sarai favored Hagar because Hagar was her slave. Thus, Sarai ensured any offspring of Abram and Sarai's slave belonged to her. On the other hand, Sarai may have chosen Hagar because she resented Hagar. As Sarai's maid in pharaoh's harem, Hagar knew that Sarai had intercourse with pharaoh. Sarai was embarrassed in front of Hagar. She chose Hagar to undergo the same experience with Abram that she had with pharaoh, i.e., compelled intercourse.

When Abram had intercourse with Hagar, she became Abram's secondary wife; but, she remained Sarai's slave. After Hagar became pregnant with Abram's child, Hagar's behavior toward Sarai changed. Hagar started to "despise" Sarai (Genesis 16:4). Despise is an ugly word that meant Hagar looked on Sarai with contempt and aversion. Hagar regarded Sarai as negligible and worthless because she couldn't conceive children. Hagar may have stated that Sarai was barren; consequently, what good was Sarai as a woman? In Abram and Sarah's minds Hagar conceived and carried a child for Sarai; however, Hagar acted like she was carrying the child for herself. Hagar role modeled disrespect for Sarai. Perhaps, Hagar even built alliances with other disgruntled servants. All showed a subtle disrespect for Sarai. Distressed by Hagar's behavior, Sarai went to Abram.

Although it was her idea for Abram to conceive a child with Hagar, Sarai blamed Abram for Hagar's behavior. Sarai demanded Abram to do something about the way Hagar treated her. Because Sarai was a smart woman, likely her demand included an appeal to the decades-long relationship between her and Abram. Sarai legitimized her demand by appealing to the Lord, who Abram followed, "May the Lord judge between you and me" (Genesis 16:5). Sarai may have used tears, i.e., manipulation.

In his response Abram used a negative influence technique, i.e., avoidance. He told Sarai, "Your slave is in your hands. Do whatever you think best" (Genesis 16:6). Abram's word choice was significant. Clearly Abram wanted to avoid conflict with Sarai and to maintain his relationship with her. Abram continued to see Hagar as Sarai's slave, not his secondary wife. Abram had no, or few, feelings for Hagar despite having intercourse with her. The outcome of Sarai and Hagar's animosity was that Sarai treated Hagar so badly (intimidation, threat, overwork) that Hagar fled Abram's camp.

Hagar's getaway took her to a spring of water in the direction of Egypt where God's angel met Hagar. The angel directed Hagar to return to Abram's camp and submit to Sarai. God planned to make Hagar's descendants so many that they couldn't be counted. Hagar followed the angel's direction and returned to the camp. We have no idea how Sarai reacted when Hagar returned. Was Sarai happy or sad? Did she punish Hagar? Did Sarai's treatment of Hagar improve or worsen? Sarai could have had Hagar killed for running away.

Sarai's reason for allowing Hagar to live was likely because Hagar carried Abram child.

Because Hagar's child belonged to Sarai, Sarai would/should have been at the birth. In many instances, the birth mother leaned on the legs of the adoptive mother as the baby left her body. This position showed she was giving birth for the adoptive mother. Despite Hagar birthing Ishmael for Sarai, Hagar remained Ishmael's mother figure. She provided Ishmael with breast milk. The Bible narrative suggested that Sarah didn't treat Ishmael as she would have treated a son from her own body. Despite Sarai's treatment of Ishmael, Abram considered Ishmael his son.

Abram was 86 and Sarai 76 years old when Hagar birthed Ishmael. Ishmael means "God hears." Because God heard, didn't mean that God agreed with Sarai and Abram's solution. Not for another 14-15 years did God again visit Abram. In a fifth visit, God repeated that he would give Abram the entire land of Canaan and make him fruitful. God changed Abram's name to Abraham and Sarai's name to Sarah. God told Abraham that Sarah, not Hagar, would be the mother of his descendants. When God told Abraham he would father a son with Sarah, Abraham laughed. Abraham was almost 100 and Sarah in her late 80s. Realistically, they weren't going to have a son at those ages.

When Abraham told Sarah God's revelation, she was skeptical. Possibly, she even attempted to influence Abraham to doubt God's promise. Likely Sarah used the influence technique consulting. With consulting the individual (influencer) asks questions to get the other person (influencee, target) to agree with them. Sarah could have asked: Why did God only now identify her as mother of this new nation? Why didn't God tell Abraham 24 years earlier that Sarah would give birth to a son? Did God discount Sarah's yearning to be a mother? Why didn't God speak directly to Sarah?

Perhaps God's goal was for Sarah to accept that she was as important as Abraham to his plan to build a holy nation. Promises God made to Abraham were made to Sarah. In God's perspective Sarah and Abraham were one flesh—husband and wife. What God told one, he told both. Somewhere over the past two decades, Sarah forgot that as Abraham's wife, she was vital to creation of a nation that would worship God.

What happened next must have shocked both Sarah and Abraham. In preparation for a pregnancy, Sarah's body changed. She again produced female hormones (estrogen and progesterone) so she could become fertile, i.e., her ovaries produce an ovum each month. Sarah's uterus became receptive for a fertilized ovum. Her breast, once saggy and without texture, become firm and round as they prepared to produce milk for a new born. With the production of female sex hormones Sarah's skin became soft and elastic, wrinkles disappeared. Despite being 89 years-old, Sarah's appearance was that of an attractive, childbearing woman.

During the months Sarah's body changed to accept a baby, Abraham moved the family from Hebron to the vicinity of Gerar. Sarah was so attractive that Abraham feared that Gerar's king would kill him to acquire Sarah. Again, Abraham lied and told everyone that Sarah was his sister. Why did Sarah make no effort to influence Abraham to acknowledge her as his wife? Perhaps dejectedly, Sarah thought, "Why bother?" Despite her body changes, Sarah continued to feel inadequate as wife to the very wealthy Abraham. Because Abraham had Ishmael, would Abraham divorce her if she spoke up and opposed what Abraham wanted done?

Abimelech, the king of Gerar, took Sarah into his harem with the intention of making Sarah his wife. Unlike the story of pharaoh in Egypt, the Bible recorded that Abimelech never had sexual intercourse with Sarah. In a dream, God told King Abimelech that Sarah was Abraham's wife and Abimelech must return her to Abraham. King Abimelech called Abraham to account for his actions. Abraham admitted that he lied about his relationship with Sarah. His reason was that he feared King Abimelech would kill him to acquire Sarah. Similar to the situation in Egypt, Abraham put his personal safety before that of his wife's honor. Sarah's beauty (attraction power) influenced the normally-righteous Abraham to lie again.

Twenty-five years after God first appeared to Abraham and promised that he would be the father of a great nation, Abraham and Sarah had a son. Abraham was 100 and Sarah was 90 years-old. The elderly couple named their son, Isaac, "he laughs." Both Abraham and Sarah's laughter of disbelief became the laughter of joy. Probably, Sarah couldn't let Isaac out of her arms or out of her sight. When Isaac was weaned—usually at about three years of age—Abraham had a great feast.

At this time Ishmael was 16-17 years-of-age. Both Ishmael and Hagar were jealous at the attention Isaac received. At the festival Sarah saw Hagar and Ishmael laughing (mocking) at Isaac. Sarah became angry. She demanded that Abraham send Hagar and Ishmael away from the camp. I wonder what influence technique Sarah used to persuade Abraham to act so drastically. Did Sarah appeal to God's words (legitimizing) that Isaac, not Ishmael, would be the father of this new nation of God-worshipers? Maybe Sarah used consulting. She questioned how Isaac could be head of the family after Abraham when Ishmael was Abraham first-born son. Ishmael had an almost twenty year history of being Abraham's son among Abraham's people.

Sarah's efforts displeased Abraham, not so much because Hagar would be sent away, but because his son, Ishmael, would be expelled. Nonetheless, Abraham obeyed when God told Abraham to attend to Sarah's words. God's blessing of Abraham's offspring would be through Isaac. God assured Abraham that he would continue to watch over Ishmael. The next morning Abraham rose early, gave bread and a filled water skin to Hagar, and sent her and Ishmael away.

The way Abraham treated his secondary wife and his first-born son was questionable. Abraham sent Hagar and Ishmael off with only bread and water. Why didn't Abraham give them a donkey for Hagar to ride, a flock of sheep, and a variety of foods? Abraham had enormous wealth. Surely, he could have shared some with Hagar and Ishmael. Because Ishmael was in his mid-to-late teens, he knew how to tended flocks of sheep or goats.

Abraham broke the custom of the ancient Near East to care for his secondary wife. Further, as Abraham's son, even the son of a concubine, Ishmael should have had a share of Abraham's wealth. Abraham's apparent stingy behavior could have had three possible causes. First, he was angry that Ishmael and Hagar mocked Isaac at his weaning ceremony. Second, Abraham was so heart-sick at loosing Ishmael that he wasn't thinking straight. Third, Sarah influenced Abraham to retain his wealth for Isaac. Possible influence techniques that Sarah used were reminding Abraham that God said that Isaac was to be the heir (legitimizing). She may have reminded Abraham of their long history together and shared values; thus, Abraham should respect Sarah's opinion. Further, Abraham, Sarah, and Isaac were a different nationality with different customs and values from nations around them to include Egypt. Sarah may have used negative influence techniques, such as manipulation, in her effort to convince Abraham to do as she recommended.

Years later, when God directed Abraham to take Isaac to Mount Moriah and sacrifice him, Abraham didn't tell Sarah. Abraham concluded rightly that Sarah would object strenuously and try to influence Abraham to disobey God. Abraham left camp the day after he received God's instruction to sacrifice Isaac. Very likely, Sarah didn't share Abraham's view that God could do anything, even bring a sacrificed son back to life.

The next Bible entry about Sarah recorded her death at age 127 at Hebron. With the exception of about 20 years when Hagar was Abraham's secondary wife, Sarah was Abraham's only wife. After Sarah died, Abraham mourned and wept. Abraham purchased a special burial site for Sarah's body. He told Isaac that he wanted to be buried with Sarah. When Sarah died, Isaac was in his late 30s.

After Sarah died and Isaac married Rebekah, Abraham remarried. His new wife's name was Keturah (Genesis 25:1-6). She was a young, fertile woman. Her marriage to Abraham resulted in six sons. Possibly, the relationship between Abraham and Keturah included love; but, it was a different love from the obsession that Abraham felt for Sarah. Even after her death, Sarah influenced Abraham's actions, i.e., Abraham sent Keturah's sons from his camp so they wouldn't challenge Isaac's role as Abraham's heir. In contrast to the way Abraham expelled Hagar and Ishmael, Abraham gave Keturah's sons gifts when he sent them from the camp.

Conclusion

With the exception of God, Sarah influenced Abraham more than anyone else during his adult life. Sarah was indeed the mother of the Jews and by extension Christians who were in-grafted into the promises that God made to Abraham and Sarah (Romans 11:16-24). Sarah was neither weak nor weak-willed. We see her life over 60 plus years as she walked side-by-side with Abraham. Sarah traveled thousands of miles with Abraham as they moved at God's direction or to locate pastures for their flocks. Just as Abraham protected Sarah with his physical strength and wealth, Sarah protected Abraham with words and actions. Sarah posed twice, as Abraham's sister to reduce the possibility that Abraham would be killed by a powerful ruler.

Initially, Sarah believed God's promise that Abraham and she would be the parents of a nation that God chose as his special people. Years later Sarah went through a period of unbelief. During that period of time, Sarah arranged for Abraham to take a secondary wife. Abraham fathered Ishmael. Finally, Sarah found her faith in God once again. She had her God-promised son and could be the mother of a nation.

Chapter 7

Moses' Mothers and Wives

Exodus chapters 1-4; Numbers 12:1-2

Chapter 7 is largely about the women who were Moses' mothers and wives. All were taken from the Bible with the exception of Tharbis, Moses' Cushite wife. Her story was documented by Josephus, the great Jewish historian, and validated by the Bible.[g] Because of women, Moses lived when many other newborn Israelite males were killed. Because of a woman, Moses won the Egyptian-Cushite war. Because of a woman, Moses had the education and military preparation to lead the Israelites out of Egypt. Because of a woman, Moses had sons. Other than God, women were the greatest influencers in Moses' life.

About 1876 BC, Jacob, his offspring, and possessions entered Egypt. Jacob's 11th son, Joseph, was a high ranking official in Egypt. Pharaoh gave the Israelites the near-empty land of Goshen for their flocks. For approximately three and one-half centuries, the Israelites lived relatively isolated from the Egyptians. The Israelites population grew in number from the approximate seventy who entered Egypt to a few million people. Egyptians began to envy their wealth. Eventually, a new pharaonic dynasty came into power which didn't know Joseph's contribution to Egypt and to the pharaoh's power. When the new pharaoh saw the number of Israelite foreigners who lived in Egypt, he feared they would join with an invading enemy army and overthrow his government.

Pharaoh made the Israelites slaves, set hard task masters over them, and worked them tirelessly. Despite the harsh labor, the Israelites continued to multiply. The Bible's exact words were, "the more they were oppressed, the more they multiplied and the more they spread abroad" (Exodus 1:12). When pharaoh saw that slave labor didn't reduce the number of Israelite births, he called in the Israelite midwives. Two Israelite midwives were named, Shiphrah and Puah. Pharaoh gave the two midwives orders to kill all newborn Israelite sons they helped to deliver; girls could live.

Imagine a ruler telling two women whose vocation was to bring life into the world, to kill newborn babies! Naturally, the midwives disobeyed pharaoh. They allowed Israelite newborn sons, as well as daughters, to live. Again, pharaoh called the two midwives before him. Pharaoh asked the midwives why they allowed the male children to live. In their response, the midwives lied to pharaoh. They said that Israelite women were so vigorous that they gave birth before the midwives could get to their homes to aid delivery of their babies. By stating a lie as truth, the two midwives saved Moses' life at his birth.

Moses' Birth Mother

Despite the midwives actions, pharaoh remained adamant about reducing the size of the Israelite population. His next edict was that every son born to an Israelite woman must be thrown into the Nile River; again new-born daughters could live. Amram and Jochebed were a married couple from the tribe of Levi. Amram means "exalted people," while Jochebed means "the honor of Jehovah." Given that both Amram and Jochebed had spiritual-sounding names, they were an Israelite remnant who believed in the God of Abraham, Isaac, and Jacob. Apparently, their marriage was successful despite their status as slaves.

In this difficult environment, Jochebed became pregnant. The couple already had two children: Aaron was about three years-old, Miriam about seven years-old. Amram and Jochebed knew that if Jochebed delivered a son, they were required by pharaoh's edict to put him into the Nile River. There, the new born would drown or be eaten by a predator. If they didn't put the newborn son into the Nile River, someone would report them to the Egyptians. Not only would the Egyptians kill the neonate, likely they would kill Amram, Jochebed, and their other two children.

When Moses was born, Amram and Jochebed were unified in their decision not to place him in the Nile River to drown. They hide Moses in their home. After three months neighbors could hear the infant's cries. More ominous, any nearby Egyptians could hear the baby's cries. What should Amram and Jochebed do? As slaves they had no power and no influence.

Can you imagine Amram and Jochebed sitting up late into the night—even though Amram was exhausted by daily slave labor—exploring every option for saving their newborn son? Finally, they evolved a strategy. Like all slaves in the area, they knew where pharaoh's daughter bathed in the Nile River. They determined to place their newborn son in a floating basket (ark) near the bathing site. Perhaps, the princess would see the basket among the Nile reeds and save their son's life. Alternatively, both parents knew the royal princess could just as easily ignore the baby or have her father's soldiers murder him.

Amram went to work each morning. At home Jochebed created a cradle of papyrus reeds. She covered it with bitumen (tar) so it would float. Making the cradle, covering it with tar, and allowing the tar to dry took several days. Finally, the day came when Jochebed had to place Moses in the cradle and the cradle in the Nile River. Likely, that morning Amram took one last looked at their son, kissed him, and left the house for his long day of slave labor.

Jochebed placed Moses in the basket, floated the basket in the Nile River, and went home. Jochebed hope that pharaoh's daughter would find the floating basket near her bathing site. She prayed that the royal daughter shared her belief that a newborn child was innocent and deserved life. Jochebed's love for her son was so great that she decided to allow a woman from a different nation, religion, and culture to rear him. She accepted that Moses would call this other woman "Mother." Jochebed was the premier role model of a Bible woman, who loved her new-born child.

Moses' Royal Mother

Pharaoh's daughter and attendants went to the Nile River to bathe. As they walked along the river's edge, pharaoh's daughter saw a basket floating among the Nile River reeds. The royal daughter sent attendants to fetch the basket. When she opened it, the royal daughter saw a crying baby. She recognized that he was a Hebrew baby. Her recognition could have resulted from the distinctive designs of the baby's clothing and blankets, or because Hebrew skin color and facial patterns were different from those of Egyptians.

The royal princess knew her father's edict that all male Hebrew babies be thrown into the Nile River. She knew the fate of those abandoned babies. This was the moment of truth. Would pharaoh's daughter order the bulrush basket returned to the Nile River, her father's soldiers to kill the baby, or would she protect the baby? Pharaoh's daughter determined to keep the baby. Miriam watched the floating basket from a short distance away. She stepped forward and volunteered to find a Hebrew wet nurse for the infant. When pharaoh's daughter agreed, Miriam ran home and brought Jochebed back.

The biblical account of pharaoh's daughter retrieving Moses from the Nile River and hiring his mother to nurse him provides scant information about this royal princess. Bible and Egyptian scholars proposed several names for her. The great first century Jewish historian, Josephus, offered that the pharaoh's daughter was Thermuthis.[8] Josephus wrote that when Thermuthis saw the infant in the basket, she loved him immediately. More recent scholars suggested that the Egyptian princess was Hatshepsut.[9] She was the only daughter of the reigning pharaoh. Hatshepsut could have been as young as 6-7 years-old. Hatshepsut knew that her father ordered all Israelite male babies killed; yet, even as a young girl, she was strong. She wanted this baby. Likely Hatshepsut used a number of influence techniques, i.e., persuading, appeal to the father-daughter relationship, even manipulation, to convince her powerful father to allow her to keep the child.

Pharaoh's daughter named the infant Moses which means "I drew him out of the water." She paid Jochebed to breast feed Moses. Jochebed may have breast fed Moses until he was in his third year-of-life. After Moses was weaned, pharaoh's daughter took Moses into the Egyptian royal household. For the next 37 years Moses was cared for and educated as the son of pharaoh's daughter. He had all the privileges of a son in the royal court.

We will never know the types of power and number of influence techniques the royal princess used to keep Moses alive and to ensure that he received the best education and training available. Rational influence techniques likely included legitimizing or appealing to her father's authority to keep Moses safe. Repeatedly, she claimed (stated) that Moses was her son. Social influence techniques she used most likely included socializing with other royal family members and building relationship with them so they would support her cause. The royal princess used alliance building to find other supporters. In turn these allies used their influence with pharaoh to keep Moses alive and to ensure he received the rights and privileges of a royal son. Very likely, this princess used negative influence techniques, such as manipulation and intimidation, against those who opposed her.

A Cushite Wife

Miriam identified that Moses had a "Cushite wife" (Numbers 12:1-2); but the Bible is otherwise silent on whether or not Moses married a Cushite woman. Possibly, Moses' Cushite wife was Zipporah, the wife who Moses married while he lived with the Midianites (Exodus chapter 2). The problem with this interpretation is that the physical appearance of people who lived in Cush and Midian differed. Cush, known today as Ethiopia, was a country south of Egypt inhabited by offspring of Ham, the second son of Noah. The Cushites were a dark-skinned race. In contrast to the Cushites, Midianites were Semites, offspring of Noah's son Shem. Their skin was only a little, or no darker, than the Israelites. Midian was a son of Abraham by his wife Keturah. Midianite land was on the northwestern side of the Arabian Peninsula, not in Africa.

According to the Jewish historian, Josephus, Moses married an Ethiopian princess.[8] In *Antiquity of Jews*, Josephus recorded that pharaoh appointed Moses as commander of the Egyptian army near the end of a largely unsuccessful war against the Ethiopians. Moses was educated in battle strategy as well as physical combat (Acts 7:22). This assignment—commander of the Egyptian army—was congruent with being a son of pharaoh.

In the war between Egypt and Cush, Moses reclaimed many Egyptian towns and cities lost to Ethiopia in earlier battles. Eventually, the Ethiopian army retreated to Saba (Meroe) their capital city. Saba was virtually impregnable from the outside. One day, Moses led an attack against the city. While he was fighting, Tharbis, daughter of the Ethiopian king, saw Moses. She fell in love with him. Tharbis sent word to Moses through a trusted servant that she would deliver the city to him if Moses agreed to marry her. After

Moses took an oath to marry Tharbis, she told Moses how he could capture Saba. After Moses captured Saba, he married Tharbis, an Ethiopian (Cushite) princess.

Imagine the inherent power and influence of Tharbis. She was a Cushite princess so her every utterance was obeyed in the royal palace in Saba. She was influential in Moses' success as a military leader. She negotiated with Moses to turn the royal city over to him, if he would marry her. Consider the expense, manpower, and loss of life that would have resulted from Moses' continued siege of Saba. Possibly, Moses and the Egyptian army would never have been able to overcome the defenses of Saba. In contrast to that dire scenario, Tharbis handed Moses a secret way into the city. Through Tharbis's influence, Moses defeated the Cushites after all other Egyptian war commanders failed to win the Egypt-Cush war.

Probably, Moses was in his 20s or early 30s when he married Tharbis. Likely Moses brought his Ethiopian bride to his Egyptian mother and to pharaoh's royal court. There is no information to suggest that Moses had offspring with Tharbis. When Moses killed an Egyptian and fled Egypt, he didn't take Tharbis with him. He abandoned his Cushite wife in Egypt. More than likely Tharbis remained under the care and protection of Moses' Egyptian mother.

Tharbis loved Moses. She remained his wife for the 40 years he was in Midian. As Moses' wife Tharbis left Egypt with Moses during the exodus. When Miriam criticized Moses for having a Cushite wife, the Israelites were camped at Hazeroth on the Sinai Peninsula. By this time the Tabernacle was dedicated, God anointed seventy elders to assist Moses with management of the Israelites, and God began to feed the Israelites with manna. Seemingly, Tharbis was a presence in the Israelite camp for years. Whether or not Tharbis influenced Moses during the exodus is unknown, but she was powerful enough to threaten or intimidate Moses' sister, Miriam, who singled Tharbis out for criticism.

Zipporah, Mother of Moses' Sons

After Moses killed an Egyptian, he fled to Midian, an area outside Egypt's control and influence. When Moses came to Midian, he sat down beside a well. In the Midian area, Jethro was a priest. He had seven daughters. Daily, Jethro's daughters brought their flock to the well for water. Moses saw other shepherds attempt to drive the girls away from the well. He rescued the girls and drew water for their sheep. When Jethro learned of Moses' rescue, he invited Moses to eat with him. Moses stayed with Jethro. Later, Moses married Jethro's daughter, Zipporah. Zipporah's name means "bird" which could allude to her beauty, or quickness of action. Moses and Zipporah had two sons. The first was named Gershom ("alien"); the second was named Eliezer ("my God is helper") (Exodus 18:3-4).

After Moses lived with Jethro's family about 40 years, God ordered Moses to return to Egypt. God told Moses to lead the Israelites out of Egypt and into the land God promised to Abraham, i.e., Canaan. Somewhat reluctantly, Moses agreed to God's plan. He took Zipporah and their two sons and started back to Egypt. On the way, God met Moses at a lodging place and made Moses acutely, almost fatally, ill. Zipporah recognized that God's wrath against Moses was because he failed to circumcise one of his sons. Instantly, she circumcised that son. Zipporah's quick action turned God's wrath away from Moses. Moses survived this meeting with God only because of Zipporah's intervention.

Somewhere on their journey from Midian to Egypt, Moses sent Zipporah and their sons back to Jethro. Possibly, the point was when Zipporah circumcised her son. Immediately following the circumcision, Moses' son wasn't able to travel. Meticulous about obeying God, Moses went forward to Egypt. As logical as this scenario sounds, Rabbi Judah Law proposed another scenario.[10] Rabbi Law wrote that when Aaron met Moses on Mount Horeb, Aaron convinced Moses to send Zipporah and sons back to Midian. Rabbi Law didn't give reasons for Aaron's advice; however, three reasons come to mind. First, pharaoh could use Zipporah and sons as pawns in his conflict with Moses. Second, taking the family into Egypt would cause them needless hardship as Moses and Aaron attempted to get the Israelite slaves free from their Egyptian masters.

Despite these two logical reasons for Moses sending his family back to Midian, another reason is equally plausible. Aaron brought Moses the unexpected news that his Cushite wife still lived in Egypt. Moses wasn't ready for his two wives to meet. He didn't want the distraction of dealing with two wives while he convinced pharaoh to give the Israelites their freedom. When Moses married Zipporah, he didn't expect to return to Egypt or again see Tharbis. After living 40 years with Jethro and the Midianites, Moses surmised that Tharbis died, divorced him, or returned to Cush. Fortunately or unfortunately, Tharbis was very much alive and living in Egypt when Moses returned to Egypt to lead the Israelite exodus.

While the Israelites were camped at Mount Sinai, Jethro brought Zipporah and Moses' two sons to Moses (Exodus 18:1-8). After Zipporah's arrival, Moses had two wives in the Israelite camp, i.e., Tharbis, the Cushite princess, and Zipporah, the Midianite daughter of Jethro and mother of Moses' sons. In ancient Egypt polygamy was acceptable; however, only very wealthy individuals could afford more than one wife. If a man had more than one wife, one was the "chief" wife. Neither the Bible nor Josephus indicated whether Tharbis or Zipporah were Moses' chief wife, assuming both were married to him at the same time.

The writer of Genesis through Deuteronomy was Moses; Moses implied that he lived alone in the Israelite camp. The Bible didn't record when Tharbis and Zipporah died or where each was buried. After the Israelite exodus from Egypt, often Moses referred to Zipporah, not as his wife, but as "Zipporah and her sons" By using this descriptor, Moses distanced himself from his Midianite wife.

Conclusion

Without the power and influence of the women midwives, Moses would have died at birth. He had two mothers and two wives. Each woman had power and each influenced Moses' life. Without Jochebed Moses would have died shortly after his birth. Because of his royal mother, Moses was educated as a royal son in the most advanced kingdom in the ancient Near East. Because of a woman, Moses succeeded in Egyptian-Cushite battles where other commanders failed. Because of a woman, Moses had two sons and God didn't kill him for disobedience on his way back to Egypt.

Moses wrote the book of Exodus where descriptions of his birth, mothers, and wives were recorded in the Bible. Few of these descriptions were complete. Perhaps the lack of information was due to Moses' modesty about his personal life, but, there are several other explanations about this dearth of information from Moses. Perhaps, Moses remembered little about Jochebed; consequently, he wrote little about her. Jochebed could have been completely out of Moses' life after he was three years-old. Out of gratitude toward his royal mother and his pharaoh grandfather, Moses didn't identify them. After all, this pharaoh enslaved and killed Israelites living in Egypt. The absence or lack of information on Tharbis and Zipporah could have been because neither were Israelites. Tharbis was a Cushite and Zipporah a Midianite. Nationalistic Israelites considered both women as aliens. Moses could have been embarrassed to be married to two women, neither of whom were Israelites.

If none, some, or all of these reasons contributed to the lack of a complete picture of Moses' mothers and wives, the women were still part of his life. Moses' mothers influenced his feelings and thoughts from a child through adulthood. His wives were part of his successes in Egypt and in the wilderness.

Chapter 8

Deborah, Tower of Influence

Judges chapters 4 and 5

Judges, the sixth book in the Bible, is replete with the subtle and not-so-subtle influence of women. The time period was approximately 325 years (1375-1050 BC). During the era of Israelite judges, the newly-settled Israelites were primarily farmers and small artisans (weavers, dyers, smiths, potters). Power was held by clan and tribal elders assisted by regional judges (*shofetim*). In theory, the Israelites united against outside military threats. At the same time, few, if any, tribes had standing armies. Israelites almost never trained for war. Scathingly, Josephus wrote that after the Israelites entered the Promised Land, they became effeminate and lost military knowledge and skill.[8]

In virtually every Israelite tribe or region, the following pattern occurred:

- The Israelite's lapsed into idolatry
- The Israelites were defeated or over-run, by a foreign enemy, or by indigenous people who the Israelites failed to destroy when they conquered Canaan
- The Israelites repented and cried out to God after years of suppression
- God raised a judge who through a battle or battles threw off the tyranny of the suppressor and freed the Israelites
- The Israelites remained loyal to God for a time, usually the life of the judge
- After the judge's death, the Israelites relapsed into idolatry

Deborah was a wife, prophetesses, and the only female judge identified in the Bible. The name Deborah means "bee" or "honey bee." She could have been named Deborah at her birth; but more than likely she was given the name later in her life. Deborah could have gotten her name several ways. First, Israelites swarmed (like bees), or came, to Deborah when she functioned as judge in Ephraim. Second, the men of Israel swarmed (or followed) behind Deborah and Barak in the battle against King Jabin's army. Finally, in ancient Israel dates from palm trees were used to make honey syrup. Bees pollinate date flowers. Possibly, bees constantly buzzed around the palm tree where Deborah held court.

Deborah's power was largely positional. Although a wife, Deborah's power didn't come from her position as wife or her relationship with her husband. The Bible recorded scant information about Deborah's husband and even less about Deborah's role within the home. Deborah's husband was named Lappidoth. From the Hebrew language Lappidoth is translated as "torches" or "lightning" flashes." His name suggested that Lappidoth illuminated Deborah's thoughts. Although Deborah is called a "mother in Israel," no offspring were associated with her and Lappidoth. Possibly, "mother in Israel" denoted her symbolic caring for the Israelites. Alternatively, and probably less likely, Deborah became a judge after her children were grown.

The Bible never recorded that Deborah was attractive or charismatic. Although she may have been both, Deborah's power came from her role as God's judge. Deborah lived in Ephraim. She held court in a fixed location, under a palm tree (Palm of Deborah) in the Ephraim hill country between Ramah and Bethel. At this time in Israel, judges had two functions: (a) administer justice largely through ajudicating disputes and (b) lead Israelite armies in battle. Although Deborah was identified as the fifth Israelite judge in the Promised Land, she didn't lead the Israelite army. God instructed Deborah to use Barak to command the Israelite army to throw off Canaanite suppression of the Israelites. Both God and Deborah knew that although the Israelites would accept a woman arbitrating disputes, they wouldn't accept one as commander of an army in battle.

As an Israelite judge, Deborah had to know Mosaic Law, primarily laws set forth in Deuteronomy. During the years that Deborah served as judge, few men and fewer women could read or write. Yet, Deborah knew Mosaic Law including its implications (knowledge power). According to Deuteronomy, judges were to hear cases between Israelites and between aliens and Israelites (Deuteronomy

1:16). The judge was to listen to both sides of the argument and investigate it thoroughly (Deuteronomy 19:18). An Israelite judge wasn't permitted to show partiality in judgment, i.e., give the rich and powerful more favorable rulings than the poor (Deuteronomy 1:17). If the case was too difficult for the judge to decide, he/she took it to God who gave the judge a ruling. Once Israelites brought a case to a judge to settle, they were expected to follow the judge's verdict (Deuteronomy 17:11).

Because she was a judge over Israel, Deborah had network power. Likely, leaders of many clans in Ephraim and even beyond Ephraim brought their cases to Deborah to decide. Deborah got information from petitioners. She learned where and how the Kishon River flowed and where Mount Tabor was located in relation to Hazor, Jabin's strong hold. She learned that Commander Sisera garrisoned his army at Harosheth Haggoyim, southwest of the Kishon River. Deborah knew that when rainfall was particularly heavy, the Kishon River flooded the Jezreel Valley. Over time Deborah learned this information and much more. She never imagined the information would be useful to her when planning a military battle.

Never once did the Bible hint that Deborah was corrupt in her judgments. She had high reputation power among the clans and tribes of Israel. As a judge Deborah's eloquence (expressive power) enhanced her overall power. She explained the rationale for judgments clearly showing her in-depth knowledge of Israelite law. Deborah's eloquence was further validated by the "The Song of Deborah" sung by Deborah and Barak after Jabin's defeat.

Deborah was God's prophetess or his spokesperson. As a prophetess Deborah relayed God's words without any interpretation or embellishment. Deborah was God's voice. The Bible didn't identify how God communicated with Deborah. She either heard his voice or had visions when she was awake or asleep. If what prophets said didn't come true, they were considered false prophets (Deuteronomy 18:20-22). Nowhere did Bible writers identify that Deborah was a false prophetess. Notice the difference between Deborah's communications as a judge versus as a prophetess. As a judge Deborah gave explanations of her interpretation of the Mosaic Law and explained how the law applied to the case in front of her. As a prophetess, Deborah relayed God's message verbatim without interpretation.[3]

By the time Deborah initiated a meeting with Barak, Israelites were oppressed for twenty years by King Jabin. King Jabin ruled from a large, well-fortified city in northern Canaan. He led a confederacy of Canaanite city-states spread throughout the central Israelite tribes. Sisera, Jabin's war commander, had 900 iron chariots in his army. To put this chariot number in perspective, the Egyptian Pharaoh Thutmose had 924 chariots in the entire Egyptian army. Israelites that lived in areas controlled by King Jubin were demoralized. They couldn't safely travel main roads. Instead they had to take winding mountainous paths to avoid enemy troops and marauders. Village life ceased as Israelites fled to walled towns for protection. Because of Jabin's army, Israelite farmers had no access to the fertile Jezreel Valley.

Deborah had power and influence over Israelites who believed in God because she spoke God's message. When Deborah sent for Barak, he made the 80 mile trip from Kedesh, Naphatali to Deborah's home in Ephraim. Barak knew Deborah's reputation, that she was God's judge and prophetess. Barak's father was a clan, not a tribal leader, in Naphtali. Barak's leadership experience was limited to small groups of men. The name Barak means "lightening" which could refer to Barak's quick actions to include quick decision-making. Perhaps Barak's ability to act quickly was an important reason that God enlisted him to make battlefield decisions.

When Barak arrived at her location, Deborah said: "The Lord, the God of Israel, commands you: "Go, take with you ten thousand men of Naphtali and Zebulun and lead them up to Mount Tabor. I will lead Sisera, the commander of Jabin's army, with his chariots and his troops to the Kishon River and give him into your hands"" (Judges 4:6-7). Notice Deborah legitimized her prophetic message to Barak by saying that the God of Israel commanded Barak to take this action. In addition, Deborah's message included "what" Barak was to do, i.e., fight a battle with Sisera, King Jabin's war commander. God gave the "where" and "how" of the battle. This battle would take place in the area of the Kishon River in the Jezreel Valley. God identified the exact number of men Barak was to recruit and which tribes they should come from. God assured Barak that he would win the battle over Sisera.

Deborah's message to Barak showed she had expressive power. Deborah was both succinct and clear as she relayed God's message to Barak. There were no excess words (filler). Likewise, God's commands didn't leave room for ambiguity or any different interpretation of what Barak should do. God told Barak to recruit 10,000 men from Naphtali and Zebulun for the Israelite army; however, men from other Israelites tribes, i.e., Ephraim, Benjamin, Manasseh, and Issachar, joined with the Israelite army against Sisera. Not infrequently when a coalition of nations, cities, or states joins together against a common enemy, network power draws other individuals/nations into the coalition. Likely, Deborah used both formal and informal network power to extend her reach into several Israelite tribes and caused these tribes to send men to bolster Barak's army.

When Deborah told Barak what God wanted him to do, she encountered resistance from Barak. Barak didn't want to accept military leadership of the Israelite army. Barak was reared in a rural area with rural manners. So was I. I had four brothers and know how rural men think and act. Barak had too much respectful for God's judge to forthrightly tell Deborah, "No way." But, I can see a 20 something year-old Barak, putting his hands in the equivalent of his jean's pockets and thinking, "You want me to do what, ma'am? How am I going to get out of this?

After some persuasion from Deborah, Barak agreed to become the leader of the Israelite army; but, he would only lead the army if Deborah went with him. Barak wanted Deborah to put her life on the line along with him. Perhaps Barak didn't trust Deborah's motives. Barak knew Deborah was a judge; but, his home and the Palm of Deborah were miles apart. Past meetings, planned or chance, between Barak and Deborah were rare if they ever occurred. Barak may have had confidence in Deborah as a judge, but had doubts about her prophetic message from God.

When we consider the era that Deborah and Barak lived in, Barak's response to Deborah's words that God commanded him to lead the Israelite army wasn't too surprising. At this time in Israelite history, only a few Israelites had first-hand experiences with God. True, they all knew the history of God leading the Israelites with fire and a pillar of smoke in the desert. They knew that God was instrumental in the Israelites conquering Jericho and in Joshua's initial military victories in the Promised Land. But, in the past 200 plus years, God only interacted rarely with Israelites. Further, Barak may have considered the military advantage of 900 iron horse-drawn chariots over a poorly armed and poorly trained Israelite army.

Deborah was stunned by Barak's reluctance to follow God's plan. Her first thought may have been "How can you even think to negotiate with God's messenger?" From a stunned response, Deborah, who saw just about every type of behavior in her years as judge, turned her mind to strategies to influence Barak to obey God. Deborah would have used a mix of rational, social, and emotional influence techniques. I can imagine a middle-age Deborah looking Barak straight in the eyes and stating to Barak that he was God's choice to lead the Israelite army. She would have legitimized her position by appealing to God's authority over Barak and Israel. Clearly, Deborah used exchanging (negotiating or trading for cooperation) with Barak because she agreed to go with him to the battle. Calmly, Deborah told Barak that because of his reluctance to obey God, he wouldn't receive the honor of killing Sisera. That honor would go to a woman. At this point in Barak's negotiation with Deborah, I doubt that Barak cared who got the credit for killing Sisera.

All we read about Deborah in the book of judges, showed that she was a rational woman who used rational influence techniques; yet, I believe that Deborah used social and emotional influence techniques as well. By this time in her tenure as a judge and prophetess, she had many network contacts. Deborah consulted with these network contacts to solve problems that could occur in the upcoming battle.

Consulting is a common social influence technique. Consulting involves asking individuals question to involve them in problem solving. Very likely Deborah used consulting with Barak and other tribesmen whose support she needed in any battle against Sisera. Some question Deborah may have asked were: "What happens when the Kishon River floods the Jezreel Valley? Because of the iron on the chariots were they heavy? Will chariots get mired in the mud if the Kishon River floods?" By answering these types of questions, Barak and other tribesmen became involved in developing fighting strategies to beat the Canaanites. Further, and perhaps more importantly, they began to believe that they could win this upcoming battle with the Canaanites.

Appealing to values is an emotional influence technique that is often used by religious leaders and Deborah likely used it to induce Barak to be the Israelite commander. By appealing to Barak's values that the Israelites never again be slaves nor live in fear, Deborah built commitment in Barak for the role of commander of Israel's forces. Deborah appealed to Barak's values by reminding him of Jacob's blessing on Naphtali. That blessing included that Naphtali was to flourish (Genesis 49:21). Living under King Jabin's severe yoke of oppression meant that Naphtali couldn't flourish. The tribe was never meant to live this way.

How do you visualize Deborah? I see a middle-aged woman with upright posture. Her clothes weren't flamboyant. Her shoes were utilitarian, rather than stylish (I think of her wearing comfortable Birkenstock © sandals). She was severe in her appearance, but not aesthetic. She knew what she planned to say before she opened her mouth. Deborah had will power which she used at God's direction. Deborah made moral choices each day of her life and lived with the results without whining. Her desires and concurrent actions to achieve those desires weren't for herself, or for selfish reasons. Rather, Deborah's will power was used to enhance reverence for God among the Israelites.

The hill country of Ephraim where Deborah held court was far away from Hazor where King Jabin had his palace. Likely, King Jabin had little interest in how townsmen and villagers in Ephraim's hill country lived. Deborah could have lived quietly with Israelites coming to her several times a month for her judgements. Instead Deborah responded to God's direction. She moved out of her comfort zone. She lent her considerable character power and reputation power to the planned battle between Barak and Sisera.

Barak gathered the Israelite troops on Mount Tabor in the Jezreel Valley; 10,000 Israelite men from the central tribes of Israel were with Barak. God lured Sisera to the Jezreel Valley by allowing him to learn that Barak's army was camped on Mount Tabor. Have you ever wondered if Sisera knew that an Israelite judge was with the Israelite army? Was Sisera worried that Deborah had power—maybe she would perform a miracle—that could influence the battle outcome? Would her presence cause the Israelite soldiers to fight harder?

I don't think Deborah being with the Israelites impacted Sisera one way or the other. Sisera was absolutely confident that he could defeat the Israelites with his iron chariots. The flat Jezreel Valley was an ideal place to maximize the advantage of fast horse-drawn chariots against the Israelite foot soldiers. At the same time, the Israelite soldiers were more confident because God's judge was with them. Deborah's presence influenced Barak and his army to fight harder. They remember past victories when a judge led, or was with, an Israelite army.

Probably, Deborah didn't go onto the actual battle field, but watched the slaughter unfold from the top or side of Mount Tabor. That day God caused a heavy down pour of rain. The Kishon River flooded. Land on both sides of the river turned into an impassable quagmire. Sisera's chariots couldn't maneuver. They got stuck in the mud; soldiers had to abandon their chariots. Israelite soldiers killed most of the Canaanite troops.

Sisera abandoned his own chariot and fled on foot toward his stronghold at Harosheth Haggoyim. On the way, Sisera came to the Kenite camp of Heber, an ally of King Jabin. Heber wasn't at home; but, Heber's wife, Jael, invited Sisera to rest in her tent. Believing he was secure with known allies, Sisera fell into an exhausted sleep. While Sisera slept, Jael killed him by driving a tent peg through his temple. Thus, Deborah's prophecy that a woman would receive credit for killing Sisera came true.

Conclusion

Deborah was one of, if not, the most powerful women in the Old Testament. She had positional power, i.e., role, character, reputation, network, and information power. Because of her power she was able to influence or persuade Barak to be Israel's military commander against King Jabin and Sisera. Clearly, Barak had his doubt about accepting this job, but accept he did because Deborah, God's judge and prophetess, went into the battle with him. Because of Deborah's network power, thousands of Israelites rallied to Barak's army.

Bacon[1] claimed that will power, believing your desires and actions are right, enhanced all other sources of power and influence. Certainly, Deborah was possessed of a strong will that caused her to take actions to free the Israelites from oppression when few others were willing to challenge the might of King Jabin and his army. Her will power kept her moving forward when she met Barak's reluctance to command the Israelite army.

In the Old Testament Hall of Faith, Barak was named as a person who through faith conquered kingdoms and administered justice for the Israelites (Hebrews 11:32-33). Deborah isn't named in the Hall of Faith, although other women were identified there. Yet, without Deborah, Barak would never have entered a battle with Sisera to free the Israelites from Canaanite oppression.

Chapter 9

Samson, Surrounded by Women

Judges chapters 13 through16

Women had power over Samson and influenced his decisions.
Samson, the last of the Israelite judges (1075-1055 BC), was from
the tribe of Dan. Samson's adversaries were the Philistines, who
ruled over certain Israelite tribes to include Dan and Judah (Judges
13:1). From adulthood until his death, Samson achieved single-
handed triumphs over the Philistines. Although Samson was a heroic
figure, his personal life was a tragedy, largely because women
influenced his decisions and behavior.

Mother

Samson's mother was in Samson's life from conception into
adulthood. The Bible didn't give her name. She was referred to as
Manoah's wife or Samson's mother. I am going to refer to her as
Mrs. Manoah. Josephus described Mrs. Manoah as a beautiful
woman. He wrote that her beauty (attraction power) resulted in
Manoah being jealous of other man who interacted with his wife.[8]
Perhaps Mrs. Manoah's beauty influenced Samson to seek out
beautiful women. Neither the Bible nor Josephus said that Samson
was handsome; however, he would have been at least attractive with
his long hair and strong body.

When the Bible narrative about Samson opened, we are given insight
into Mrs. Manoah's power and how she influenced others. She was
Manoah's only wife and seemed content in her wife role, even
though the couple was childless. At the same time when an Angel of
God visited Mrs. Manoah and told her that she and Manoah would
have a son, Mrs. Manoah was ecstatic. Generously, she ran to
Manoah and shared her new knowledge with him.

The way Manoah responded to his wife's information showed Mrs.
Manoah's character and reputation in the home and possibly in the
surrounding community. Manoah didn't placate his wife with,
"Sweetheart, you want a baby so badly that you had a vivid dream."
Manoah believed every word Mrs. Manoah said. In fact, he believed

her so thoroughly that he prayed to God to send the Angel back so they could get more information from him. Not once does the Bible indicate that Manoah wanted a second visit from the Angel so he could verify his wife's story. The Angel visited the Manoah's a second time, but gave no extra information. Apparently, the Angel believed that information he gave to one marriage partner, he gave to both. The Angel didn't need to repeat God's instructions for rearing Samson.

In the final scene in Judges Chapter 14, readers get even more insight into Mrs. Manoah's character. In this vignette, the Angel of God ascended to heaven in a sacrifice flame. Manoah became alarmed. He said that they were going to die because they saw God. Mrs. Manoah disagreed. In a forthright manner Mrs. Manoah said that if God planned to kill them, God wouldn't have visited them, told them they were going to have a son, and how to rear him. Her succinct, pragmatic response calmed Manoah.

The Angel of God told Mrs. Manoah that her son was to be a Nazirite from conception. Carrying a Nazirite in the womb meant that while Mrs. Manoah was pregnant she couldn't touch a dead body or consume any grape products, i.e., raisins, wine. After his birth Samson's parents were to rear him as a Nazarite, which included that his parents never cut Samson's hair.

Mrs. Manoah's power was based largely on the longevity of her relationship (history power) with Manoah and on her expressive power. Growing up, Samson saw the value of a strong woman's opinion. Mrs. Manoah role modeled Nazarite requirements by what she gave Samson to eat and drink. Despite his mother's influence, as an adult Samson no longer adhered to Nazirite requirements with the exception that he didn't cut his hair.

Bride

Samson ignored Mrs. Manoah's example of a powerful, influential woman when he selected a wife. Samson went to Timnah, a largely Philistine town. There, Samson saw a Philistine woman. When he returned home, Samson told his parents that he wanted the woman for his wife. Samson's parents were in agreement that Samson shouldn't marry a Philistine. They tried to influence Samson to marry a Danite, or any Israelite, woman. Probably, they quoted God's direction to Moses that Israelites shouldn't marry unbelieving foreigners because these people worshiped idols (Deuteronomy 7:3).

Samson was adamant. He wanted this woman for his wife. His exact words were, "Get her for me, for she is right in my eyes" (Judges 14:3 ESV). Likely, the young woman was very attractive; thus, she caught Samson's eye. Before Samson talked to the young woman, or knew her other than by sight, he determined to marry her.

Manoah, Mrs. Manoah, and Samson went to Timnah to meet the young woman and her family. After talking with her, Samson liked the young woman even more. In addition to her beauty, the young woman's behavior attracted Samson. The Bible didn't address the young woman's character or reputation. Perhaps these personal characteristics weren't important to Samson.

The Bible used the word "like" for Samson's feelings toward his future wife. At no point do we read that Samson "loved" the woman who became his bride. The Manoah's marriage showed love between a husband and wife; however, Samson ignored the love he saw in his parent's marriage when he chose a wife. Possibly, Samson thought that marriage to the Philistine woman would evolve into a loving relationship similar to the one he saw in his parent's marriage.

The parents arranged a marriage between the young couple. Usually, the time lapse between a betrothal and a wedding was about a year. Samson arrived at Timnah and prepared a wedding feast. In the ancient Near East marriages were celebrated with seven days of feasting. The bride's family chose thirty Philistine men to be Samson's companions for the duration of the marriage feast. During a wedding feast, wine flowed freely. Likely, Samson drank wine and ate grapes, thus, breaking the Nazirite vow to consume nothing made from grapes. He moved from his mother's values and influence into the culture of his bride.

Early in the seven-day wedding celebration, Samson proposed a riddle to the Philistines. Riddles were a common way to entertain guests in both the Philistine and Israelite cultures. Trying to figure a riddle's answer was a source of discussion and enjoyment. Samson and his Philistine guests made a wager. If Samson's thirty companions answered the riddle by the end of the feast, Samson would give each a change of clothes made from linen. If the thirty guests couldn't interpret the riddle, they must give Samson thirty changes of clothes and linen garments. Thirty changes of clothes that included linen garments was a costly wager.

By the fourth day of the wedding feast, Samson's Philistine "friends" still had no idea what Samson's riddle meant. They went to Samson's bride and threatened her. If she didn't entice the riddle's answer from Samson before the end of the marriage festival, the Philistine men would burn her father's house with her and her father in it. Naturally, Samson's Philistine bride was threatened and intimidated. She should have gone to Samson with the threat made against her and her father. Instead, Samson's bride spent the next three days cajoling Samson to learn the riddle's answer. She accused Samson of not loving her. If Samson really loved her, he would tell her the riddle's answer. After three days of refusing his bride, Samson explained the riddle to her. She took the answer to the Philistine men.

When the Philistine men gave the riddle's answer to Samson, he knew that his bride betrayed him. Yet, Samson still owed his guests the linen clothes. Samson left his bride's home, killed thirty Philistines, and plundered their bodies. He gave the dead men's garments to the thirty men who solved the riddle. Prior to killing the thirty men, the Spirit of God came upon Samson, indicating that God approved of Samson's actions (Judges 14:19).

Angry with his new bride, Samson went back to his parent's house. Although Samson's wife was attractive, she lacked character. Her loyalty remained to her father and to the Philistines, rather than to her new husband. She used the negative influence technique, manipulation, to cajole the riddle's answer from Samson. Only belatedly did Samson recognize or care about his wife's character.

Although Josephus recorded that Samson divorced his Philistine bride, the Bible doesn't provide any such information.[8] Instead, the Bible recorded that later Samson went to Timnah to be with his new bride. Her father admitted that he gave Samson's bride to another man, thinking that Samson no longer wanted her. The Philistine father's action made sense. Because his bride manipulated and betrayed Samson, why would Samson want her?

Samson was so angry over the loss of his bride, that he destroyed Philistine crops in the area. The Philistines around Timnah learned why Samson burned their crop. They retaliated against Samson's bride and her father by burning both of them to death. When Samson heard what occurred, he became even angrier. He wanted revenge on the Philistines for the murder of his wife. As a result Samson struck the Philistines hip and thigh with a great blow.

Prostitute

As we read the Bible account of Samson judgeship, not once do we read that Samson was attracted to Israelite women; however, Philistine women were irresistible to him. One day Samson went to Gaza, a thriving Philistine city in Southern Canaan. He was recognized by the people of Gaza as the Israelite strong man who did so much damage to their crops and killed many Philistine men.

Because Gaza was a port city, it teemed with prostitutes. Samson saw a prostitute who he wanted to have sex with. Likely, the prostitute was beautiful (attraction power). Samson went into the prostitute's home and spent the remainder of the day and early night with her. Because Samson only wanted a brief interlude with the prostitute, he had no interest in her character, history, knowledge, or eloquence.

About midnight Samson got up and prepared to leave the prostitute's home. She attempted to influence Samson to stay the remainder of the night for three reasons. First, prostitutes could charge clients more money when clients spent the entire night with them. She wanted all the money she could reasonably charge Samson. Second, the woman knew that the hour was late and she was unlikely to find another man this late into the evening. A third possible reason the prostitute attempted to keep Samson was to help the Philistine men get into position to capture Samson as he left her home in the morning.

Influence techniques used by the prostitute were logic, i.e., why leave now when the night is far from over? Likely she attempted to manipulate Samson by touches and compliments. Despite these actions, the prostitute cared little about Samson. If she thought about Samson as a person, she looked down on him. After all, Samson was a Danite who the Philistines conquered.

By leaving the prostitutes home in the middle of the night, Samson avoided an attack from Philistine men. Yet, Samson knew or sensed the prostitute's effort to keep him with her overnight was so Philistine men could capture him. He was angry. Samson picked up the doors of the Gaza city gate, bars and all, and dislodged the two door posts. He put the doors, bars, and posts on his shoulders and deposited them on the top of a hill outside of Gaza. The Bible gave no information that Gaza men harmed the prostitute despite her being unable to influence Samson to spend the night with her.

Lover

Samson fell in love. His love's name was Delilah. Delilah is a Semitic name; however, Delilah's actions put her firmly in the Philistine camp. Possibly, Delilah was half Israelite and half Philistine which may explain why Samson was so comfortable around her. Josephus noted that Delilah was a harlot; however, the Bible doesn't label her as such.[8] Clearly, Delilah was an opportunist. Delilah lived in the Valley of Sorek which was located between Israelite and Philistine lands. When Philistine leaders learned that Samson spent time with Delilah, five of them visited her. Each offered Delilah eleven hundred silver shekels if Delilah cajoled Samson to reveal the secret of his great strength so they could capture him.

At no point did the Bible suggestion that the Philistines used negative influence techniques, i.e., intimidation, threat, on Delilah; but possibly the Philistine leaders used both a carrot (money) and a stick in dealings with Delilah. Similar to the thirty Philistine men who threated Samson's bride, these leaders threatened to kill Delilah and her family if she didn't comply with their orders.

Not once did the Bible suggest that Delilah loved Samson. Instead, Delilah entered into an alliance with the five Philistine leaders to obtain the secret of Samson's strength. In all fairness to Delilah, fifty-five hundred silver shekels was a tremendous amount of money. That money meant that Delilah could live an independent life style. She would have sufficient funds to buy slaves or hire servants to care for all her needs.

As we read the Bible account of Samson and Delilah, they appear to be playing a game. She asked him the source of his amazing strength. Samson answered with a lie. Although Samson lied, his answers were credible which added to the impression that Samson told the truth. For example, in Samson's first response, he told Delilah that if he was tied with seven fresh braided ropes, he would become as weak as other men. Middle Eastern people used braided rope to tie down tents against strong winds and to tie camels.

The braided rope that Samson identified was made from the yitran plant (*Thymelaea hirsute*).[11] Fresh yitran wasn't easy to obtain. It didn't grow in the Sorek Valley where Delilah lived. It grew along the seashore. In the Sorek Valley, yitran available in markets was dried, not fresh. To make fresh yitran thongs, fresh yitran had to be brought from the Mediterranean Sea coast in one day's time. Plus, the yitran had to be smooth, that is without twigs, so it could be braided into a rope.

Clearly, the Philistine rulers believed Samson's answer that if he was tied with yitran rope, he wouldn't be able to break them and defend himself. They brought Delilah seven freshly braided yitran ropes. While Samson slept, Delilah tied Samson's hands with the ropes. With Philistines hiding in an adjoining room, Delilah cried out "Samson, the Philistines are upon you" (Judges 16:9). Samson snapped the yitran thongs and killed his attackers. Samson demonstrated that his strength wasn't associated with yitran rope.

After each failure, Delilah continued to badger Samson to learn the reason for his strength. Samson continued to give Delilah false answers and she continued to relay them to the Philistines. The Philistine leaders continued to believe each of Delilah's answers. Unfortunately for the conspirators, Samson fought off the Philistine attackers each time they appeared.

After three lies and three attempts on his life, a reasonable person would have concluded that Delilah was working with the Philistines. Despite Delilah's beauty, eloquence, and charm, she was in league with his enemies. Apparently, Samson didn't put the sequence of events together. Samson continued to live with or visit Delilah, blinded by his love for her. Eventually, Delilah said to Samson, "How can you say, 'I love you' when you won't confide in me" (Judges 16:15). When Delilah uttered these words, most of us think back to Samson's wife who used the same ploy, i.e., "if you loved me."

Samson didn't learn from the result of giving the riddle's answer to his bride. Samson saw no guile in Delilah or in her actions. Samson's love for Delilah coupled with her continuing badgering, wore Samson down. Finally, Samson told Delilah that he was a Nazirite, set apart to God from his birth. He had never cut his hair; and, if his head was shaved, his strength would leave him.

Again Delilah sent word to the Philistines that she had the secret to Samson's strength. Again Philistine men gathered outside Delilah's home. Gently, Delilah lulled Samson to sleep on her lap. Samson may have been drunk; otherwise he would have felt Delilah cutting his hair. After his hair was removed, Delilah called out, "Samson, the Philistines are upon you!" (Judges 16:20). Samson woke and believed that he could go out of the house and kill the Philistine attackers. Samson didn't realize that God had left him when his hair was cut. Samson's physical strength came from God. When Samson placed his love for Delilah over his devotion to God, Samson lost God's presence and strength.

Because of Delilah's betrayal of Samson, the Philistines captured him. They gouged out Samson's eyes, bound him in bronze shackles, took him to Gaza, and set him to push a grinding wheel in prison. Never again do we read about any interaction between Delilah and Samson, or between Delilah and the Philistine leaders. Was Delilah remorseful about any of her actions? How did she feel when she saw, or learned, that the Philistines gouged out Samson's eyes? Did she imagine how her proud lover must have felt, chained to a grinding stone and forced to grind grain in prison, a job usually allocated to donkeys? Alternatively, was Delilah contented with her money regardless of the way she earned it?

Conclusion

Although power is neither moral nor immoral, the women in Samson's life with the exception of Samson's mother used their power to harm this Israelite judge. Their attraction and eloquence reached out to Samson and pulled him into their sphere of influence. The women obtained knowledge about Samson's life and behavior that compromised his effectiveness as a judge over Israel. The primary influence technique women used with Samson was a negative one. They manipulated Samson, hiding their real goals and objectives. The Philistine women withheld information Samson needed to make the right decision.

The eyes that caused Samson to sin by seeing, then marrying a Philistine woman, seeing and purchasing time with a prostitute, and finally seeing and living with the beautiful Delilah, were torn from Samson's face. Never again would Samson look on the beauty of God's creation to include the beauty of a woman.

As a Christian woman, when I study how the women in Samson's life treated him, I am embarrassed for my gender. At the same time, Samson was reared in a God-fearing home. He had a superlative role model in his mother. Samson could have behaved differently than he did. It was his choice to succumb to the power and influence of self-centered women. Despite Samson's checkered behavior as a judge over Israel, he is listed in Hebrews as a hero of the faith (Hebrew 11:32).

Chapter 10

Bathsheba, Making the Best of It

2 Samuel chapters 11 and 12; 1 Kings chapters 1, 2:13-23.

Bathsheba was the female love of King David's life. He married her when he was in his late 30s, lived in Jerusalem, and ruled over all of Israel. The Bible's factual record of Bathsheba is relatively sparse and spread over several books. Many Bible accounts showed a woman who at best was naïve and at worst a victim of male exploitation. Yet, readers who put Bathsheba's actions into the cultural mores of 1010-960 BC, see a woman who became powerful. Bathsheba saw a preferred future for herself and acted to get and keep that future. She had substantial power and influence over both her husband, King David, and her son, King Solomon.

Bathsheba's Bible story began in the spring. That year David remained in Jerusalem when the Israelite army went out to fight the Ammonites. Unable to sleep one night, David walked on the palace roof. Probably, the weather was mild and the night clear, stars shone over Jerusalem. Looking down from his palace roof, David saw a woman bathing. The woman was Bathsheba and she was beautiful (attraction power).

Bathsheba was washing and purifying herself after her monthly menses, which occurred seven days after the onset of her period. Bathsheba's decision to bathe, possibly nude, where she could be seen is perplexing. Her home was in a good part of Jerusalem, but at a lower level than the royal palace. She knew the royal palace over-looked her home. She knew, or had cause to know, that anyone on a roof at a higher elevation could look down and see her activities. It was common knowledge (information power) in Jerusalem that King David didn't go out to war with his army that spring. Little thought was required for Bathsheba to conclude that King David or some courtier walked on the palace roof on a mild Jerusalem night.

On the other hand, perhaps Bathsheba bathed monthly in this same location after her menses. Bathing there was so much a part of Bathsheba's routine that she didn't think that someone at a higher elevation would look down and see her disrobed body. On this spring night, probably Bathsheba had only a small oil lamp burning while she bathed. Light and shadows played over her beautiful body.

Bathsheba wasn't a member of the Israelite royal family, but she had status, or role power, in Jerusalem. Her role power came from the men in her life. She was the daughter of Eliam and wife of Uriah the Hittite. Both Eliam and Uriah were members of David's thirty elite soldiers (2 Samuel 23:20-39). At this time Bathsheba's husband and father were out of Jerusalem fighting with the king's army. Eliam's father and Bathsheba's grandfather was Ahithophel, one of David's counselors. Ahithophel was in Jerusalem.

After seeing Bathsheba bathing, King David sent messengers to bring her to the royal palace. When Bathsheba arrived at the palace, David had intercourse with her. Because of her father and husband's status, Bathsheba could have tried to restrain David's lust or denied him even though he was the king. One way she could have attempted to influence David was appeal (legitimizing) to Mosaic Law. Both Bathsheba and David knew that Mosaic religious law and cultural norms forbid any man from forcing a married woman to have sex with him. Bathsheba could have simply stated that she didn't want to have intercourse because she loved her husband and didn't want to be disloyal sexually to him. Both Bathsheba and David remembered that Joseph denied Potiphar's wife when she tried to seduce him (Genesis 39:11-20). Joseph even fled from his master's wife. Bathsheba could have fled from King David.

David wasn't a man who lived by his emotions. He set aside his red hot anger at Nabal when Abigail begged him not to kill Nabal or Nabal's household (1 Samuel 25:23-31). If Abigail's calming words overcame David's anger at Nabal, then Bathsheba pointing out the sin in what David planned, could have cooled David's lust.

Perhaps, Bathsheba did try to influence David not to have sex with her. Bathsheba's attempt wasn't recorded in the Bible because it would make the heroic David look like a rapist. On the other hand, perhaps the power gap was just too large between the young woman, Bathsheba, and her king. Bathsheba couldn't deny King David anything he wanted to include herself.

In the days following the night Bathsheba and David spent together, David didn't call Bathsheba to him. He thought that Bathsheba would go back to her life as wife to Uriah and tell no one of their sexual interlude. King David saw Bathsheba as a one-night stand; however, Bathsheba became pregnant from intercourse with David. When Bathsheba realized she was pregnant, she was frightened. Her husband Uriah was away from Jerusalem fighting with the Israelite army. He couldn't be the father of her pending child. She could be accused of adultery and stoned. She would humiliate her entire family.

What was Bathsheba going to do? Bathsheba sent "word," possibly via a servant, to David that she was pregnant. The Bible didn't record any message back from David to Bathsheba; nonetheless, David tried to remedy the situation. He called Uriah home from the battle field. David expected Uriah to go to Bathsheba while he was home and have intercourse with her; thus, Bathsheba could claim that Uriah was the baby's father. Although Uriah came to Jerusalem at King David's command, he didn't go home or see Bathsheba. Uriah slept on the floor of the king's palace. When David asked Uriah why he didn't go to his home, Uriah's answered that his commander (Joab) and his fellow soldiers were camped in the fields. It wasn't right for him to go to his house, eat, drink, and lay with his wife.

When Uriah came from the battlefield to Jerusalem, he went immediately to the palace and reported to King David. Very few things are secret in a family, business, or court. Someone always sees and talks about other people's behavior. Individuals in the palace knew that David had the beautiful Bathsheba brought to him. They knew that David kept Bathsheba with him all or part of the night. Palace guardsmen would have been angry that King David had sex with Uriah's wife, the same Uriah who was out fighting with the Israelite army while the king lolled, securely in his palace. It isn't difficult to believe that some offended guardsman told Uriah that David had Uriah's wife brought to him.

In a final effort to hide his adultery with Bathsheba, David ordered Commander Joab to have Uriah killed on the battle field. The Bible doesn't describe how Bathsheba felt when she learned of her husband's death. Did she mourn his death because it was Israelite custom or because she loved him? One of the Jewish sages wrote that Bathsheba and Uriah's marriage was talked about throughout Jerusalem because of their love for each other. The strong, mighty warrior showed a tender love for his beautiful wife. If this story is true, Bathsheba's period of mourning for Uriah was bitter-sweet. Bitter, because Uriah was killed; sweet, because hopefully he never learned of her adultery.

Bathsheba became King David's wife after she mourned Uriah's death. Within days of the birth of Bathsheba and David's baby, the esteemed prophet, Nathan, visited David. He told David that Bathsheba's baby would die because of David's sin. Nathan's reprimand put the onus of the adultery on David rather than on Bathsheba.

Soon after Nathan delivered his message to King David, God struck the newborn son. He became acutely ill. When King David told Bathsheba that their baby would die and why, Bathsheba felt guilt, self-condemnation, dread, and, yes, even anger at King David. Why did David up-ended her beautiful world as Uriah's wife? Now her baby was going to die because of their sin. During the newborn's illness, probably Bathsheba never left the baby's side. She carried him in her arms, washed his tiny body, and tried to feed him. Her tearful prayers were unable to influence God to change his mind. The baby died.

Bathsheba's world was crushed. She was compelled to have sex with a man not her husband. Her husband was killed in battle. She was taken from her home where she was sole wife. She was placed in a women's harem as one of David's several wives and concubines. Finally, her son died. Probably, Bathsheba couldn't stop crying. How was she to cope with all of this loss? The awful part was that she contributed to these deaths when she acquiesced to sex with King David.

The Bible recorded the next episode in Bathsheba's life with few words: "David comforted his wife Bathsheba, he went to her, and lay with her" (2 Samuel 12:24). Perhaps, David gave Bathsheba some comfort, but her grief must have nearly overwhelmed her. New to David's harem, Bathsheba had few women friends to comfort her. Eliam, Bathsheba's father, was out of Jerusalem with Joab's army.

In the Bible there is no mention of Bathsheba's mother or grandmother. Her only available relative was her grandfather, Ahithophel. Ahithophel was in Jerusalem. Likely he visited Bathsheba. As they sat and talked, Bathsheba may have poured her heart out to her grandfather, i.e., how she became pregnant, Uriah's visit to Jerusalem, and his failure to come to their home. Her narrative culminated with Nathan's prophecy that her son would die and why.

"Revenge is a dish best served cold" is an American adage. Listening to his heartbroken granddaughter's narrative of rape, murder, and finally God's retribution on David by killing Bathsheba's baby, any normal grandfather would burn with anger. This may have been the moment that Ahithophel determined to become David's chief counselor and one day betray David like David betrayed Bathsheba (2 Samuel 15:31). It may have been the time that Bathsheba determined to never again be a victim. She would get and wield power both in the harem and in the royal court.

Over the next 15-20 years, Bathsheba and David had four sons. One was Solomon. Somewhere in this time period Ahithophel rose from being one of David's counselors to his chief counselor. Perhaps Bathsheba influenced David to give precedence to her grandfather, or perhaps Ahithophel was elevated as chief counselor because he was capable. Ahithophel being King David's chief counselor increased Bathsheba's information power. She learned from her grandfather critical issues facing the Israelite nation.

Bathsheba influenced King David to guarantee that Solomon would be the next king of Israel. David had sons older than Solomon with mothers who had more illustrious lineages. The influence techniques that Bathsheba used to extract this promise from David may have been both positive and negative ones, such as, logical persuasion, alliance building, and manipulation. Apparently, Bathsheba built an alliance with Nathan, the prophet, who supported Solomon as the next king of Israel. Very likely, Bathsheba built an alliance with her powerful grandfather, Ahithophel, to encourage David to name Solomon as his successor.

King David's decision to make Solomon king after him was known in the kingdom (1 Kings 1:11-14); nevertheless, when David was in his late 60s and in frail health, his son Adonijah declared himself king. Adonijah was the eldest of David's living sons. As such, Adonijah had the most legitimate claim to Israel's throne. As soon as Nathan heard that Adonijah declared himself king, Nathan went to Bathsheba. He prompted Bathsheba to go to the elderly King David and remind David of his promise to make Solomon king.

When Bathsheba went to see King David, David allowed Bathsheba to enter his room—likely his bedroom or private sitting room. Bathsheba's access to David's private rooms speaks to a history between the two of them; a history that began with compelled sex, moved to murder, marriage, and the loss of a son. Significant events such as these were often cemented in the memory of participants. Further, over the years, Bathsheba was the wife that David repeatedly turned to sexually. When Bathsheba spoke with David, about his successor, she legitimized her request by reminding David that he swore to her by the "Lord your God" that Solomon would be king after him.

King David countered Adonijah's self-proclaimed kingship by having Solomon crowned King of Israel (1 Kings 1:28-40). Solomon took his seat on the throne of Israel (1 King 1:46). At this point, Solomon could have had all contenders to the throne killed; however, Solomon was reluctant to begin his reign with murder of his brother, Adonijah. Instead Solomon warned Adonijah that as long as he proved worthy, Adonijah wouldn't be killed (1 Kings 1:53).

For a short time before David died at age 70 years, he was frail and perhaps mentally unable to manage the complex Israelite kingdom. During this time, which ended when David died, David and Solomon were co-regents. Bathsheba was both wife to King David and the mother of King Solomon. In both roles her influence was substantial; yet the Bible recorded no actions taken by her. After Solomon became king of Israel, the most influential woman in the royal court was Bathsheba, Solomon's mother.

The Queen Mother was an official position in the Davidic dynasty. Translated from the Hebrew, *gebirah* meant queen mother or great lady. The position was both powerful and influential. Often the Queen Mother was a king's chief councilor. A king had many wives, but only one mother. Have you noticed when you read stories or descriptions of Judah's kings, that their mother was almost always identified, but only rarely was a wife's name recorded? Scripture documented that the Queen Mother may have had a throne alongside her son's throne. From this throne she was counselor and intercessor to the king. In times of conquest, both the king and his mother represented royal power [2 Kings 24:12].

Soon after David's death, Prince Adonijah approached Bathsheba and asked for a favor. Adonijah was convinced that King Solomon wouldn't refuse a request from his mother. Adonijah began his petition to Bathsheba by saying that kingship of Israel should have been his. Can you just see Bathsheba raising her eyebrows at Adonijah's assertion? Certainly, Adonijah saw them! He quickly continued with the statement that the Israelite kingdom came to Solomon from the Lord. Now, Adonijah wanted Bathsheba to do one small favor him—to ask Solomon to give Abishag to Adonijah to be his wife.

Abishag was the young virgin who kept King David warm when he was elderly. She waited on and cared for King David's physical needs. Abishag was King David's concubine, or secondary wife, but she didn't have an intimate relationship with David. Abishag was with King David when both Bathsheba and Nathan approached him, elaborated on Adonijah's self-proclaimed kingship, and reminded David that he promised that Solomon would be king after him. Abishag heard David's order that Solomon be crowned king. If Abishag became Adonijah's wife, Adonijah could influence her to say that David wanted Adonijah to be king rather than Solomon. Abishag would herself become an influential woman in the Israelite court.

Bathsheba agreed to approach Solomon with Adonijah's request. Bathsheba went to King Solomon in his throne room, probably at a time when petitioners were allowed to approach the king. When Solomon saw his mother enter the room, he stood up, went to meet her, and bowed down before his mother. Then, he sat down on his throne and ordered a second throne brought for Bathsheba, so that she could be seated on his right hand. What an honor—to have the king stand, bow before you, and have a throne brought so you could be seated in his presence. By this act Solomon declared that

Bathsheba was to be given great respect. She was the most powerful woman in the land of Israel.

When Bathsheba told Solomon that she had one small request, his told her to make the request that he wouldn't refuse it. Bathsheba requested that Solomon give Abishag to Adonijah in marriage. Solomon's response to Bathsheba was "Why do you request Abishag the Shunammite for Adonijah?" (1 Kings 2:22). Solomon continued, "You might as well request the kingdom for him, after all he is my older brother." Solomon ordered the captain of his personal guard to kill Adonijah.

Although Solomon told Bathsheba that he wouldn't decline her request, he did just that. Solomon reasoned that if Adonijah married King David's last wife, his claim to the throne of Israel would be strengthened. As David's oldest living son, already Adonijah had a strong claim, perhaps even stronger than Solomon's. In Solomon's mind, Adonijah's request to wed David's last wife was an evil, dishonorable act.

Why did Bathsheba take Adonijah's request to Solomon? By this point Bathsheba was in the king's court/harem at least 30 years. She knew that Adonijah's marriage to Abishag would strengthen his claim to Israel's throne. Bathsheba remembered that years earlier in a civil war, Prince Absalom had sex with King David's ten concubines; thus, strengthened Absalom's claim to the Israelite throne. Bathsheba could have pointed out to Adonijah that Solomon would interpret his request for Abishag as a play for Israel's throne. Bathsheba could have refused to make the request to Solomon; thus, protecting Adonijah's life

I believe that Bathsheba could hardly wait to take Adonijah's request to King Solomon. Using Adonijah's request, Bathsheba showed Solomon that until Adonijah was dead, he would continue to aspire and conspire to obtain the Israelite throne. Her request on Adonijah's behalf resulted in Solomon's decision to kill Adonijah; thus, Bathsheba further secured the throne of Israel for her son Solomon.

Conclusion

David married Ahinoam, Abigail, Maacha, Haggith, Abital, and Eglah before and during the 7-1/2 years he reigned in Hebron as king of Judah. After David became king over all of Israel, he moved his capital to Jerusalem. There, he married one woman, Bathsheba. Because Bathsheba was attractive and/or because they went through emotional times together, David's relationship with Bathsheba was more than a passing interest.

In Bathsheba's initial meeting with King David she was a naïve girl and the wife of a brave soldier. Rape, murder, marriage to David, entering the king's harem, and death of a baby caused her to mature. Bathsheba took stock of what she had and that was her beauty, a personal power source. She used that beauty to keep King David coming back to her.

In the many Bible stories that included Bathsheba, not once is she disparaged. All her words and behavior were presented as positive, or at least neutral. It's tempting to think that Bathsheba was moved around by powerful men in her life; however, I believe that conclusion is a disservice to Bathsheba. When Bathsheba met David she may have been naïve; but, being a wife of a king and living in the king's harem and court taught her the workings and intrigues of palace politics. She became a woman who used her position to influence men in her life.

Chapter 11

Jezebel, Consistent Influencer

I Kings chapters 16 through 21; 2 Kings 9:30-37

King Ahab ruled (circa 874-853 BC) the ten northern tribes of the divided Israelite kingdom for 22 years. Collectively, these 10 tribes were called the Northern Kingdom and Israel. King Ahab married Jezebel as part of a military and trade alliance. We don't know if King Ahab married Jezebel before or after he became king; however, the couple had two sons, Ahaziah and Joram (Jehoram), and one daughter, Athaliah. The Bible described King Ahab as far more wicked than any king before him. Evil acts done by King Ahab were urged on by Queen Jezebel. Jezebel was the more dominant partner in the marriage.

Jezebel was a royal princess. Her father was King Ethbaal of Sidon who ruled the loosely confederated Phoenician city-states that included Tyre and Sidon. King Ethbaal was a priest of Asherah (Astarte), the primary Phoenician goddess. Asherah was represented by a limbless tree trunk often seen in a grove of trees. The tree trunk was carved into a symbolic representation of the goddess. Growing up, probably Jezebel served as Asherah's priestess. Also, Jezebel worshiped Baal, the chief male god of the Phoenicians and Canaanites. Jezebel believed that Jehovah (Yahweh) was only a local god of Israelite lands.

Soon after Ahab and Jezebel married, Jezebel persuaded Ahab to worship Baal. She influenced Ahab to build a temple dedicated to Baal in Israel's capital city. Ahab erected an altar to Baal in the temple. At Jezebel's urging Ahab made Asherah poles for Israelites to worship. Ahab abandoned God and worshiped his wife's gods. In contrast to Ahab who abandoned his God (Yahweh), Jezebel remained completely loyal to her Phoenician gods even though she lived in Israel. At the royal table Jezebel fed 450 prophets of Baal and 400 prophets of Asherah.

Most Bible readers would argue that Jezebel was beautiful. Her beauty ensnared Ahab and influenced him to follow her lead and worship her gods. Careful reading of Bible narratives demonstrated that not once was Jezebel described as beautiful or winsome. Clearly, Jezebel had power over Ahab, but that power derived from other than her attraction.

Personal power sources are knowledge, expression, attraction, character, and history (relationship). Neither 1st nor 2nd Kings provided evidence that Jezebel was sufficiently knowledgeable, expressive, or attractive to induce Ahab to worship Phoenician gods rather than Yahweh. Nor did Jezebel and Ahab have a long standing relationship, or history power, at the time when Ahab built the temple to Baal or set up Asherah poles. To some extent, Jezebel had character power but the Bible showed that Jezebel had more character flaws than assets. Her flaws drained, thereby reduced, her character power. Jezebel's character flaws included aloofness, volatility, self-focus, and sense of entitlement.

If Jezebel lacked personal power to change Ahab and Israel's court, perhaps her power derived from her position. Positional power sources were role, resources, networks, available information, and reputation. Queen Jezebel had role power because she was the wife of King Ahab. As Ahab was the most powerful man in Israel, Jezebel was the most powerful woman. High role power was closely correlated with assertiveness, self-confidence, and being authoritarian. Jezebel had all three traits. A problem for Jezebel was that she was heavy-handed when she used both her own authority and the reflected authority of Ahab. As a result, she got compliance from individuals in the Northern Kingdom, but little commitment.

Nothing in the Bible showed that Jezebel was adept at managing resources; her positional power didn't originate from exceptional resource utilization. Nor did Jezebel build up a network of colleagues (informants) within Israel or in surrounding nations, i.e. Judah, Aram. Jezebel didn't access and interpret information that would be useful to her husband. Finally, Jezebel's reputation could only be labeled "bad." She was named an idolater, prostitute, murderer, and witch.

As analyzed above, Jezebel's personal and positional power weren't strong. So why was she viewed as powerful? Why were so many Bible verses allocated to her actions? Why were citizens in Israel afraid of her? According to the renowned 20th century theologian Herbert Lockyer,[3] Jezebel was no ordinary woman because of her will power. Her will power coupled with her strong intellect destroyed King Ahab. Her will power furthered the destruction of Israel because Jezebel led the kingdom to extravagant idolatry. Lockyer[3] wrote that Baal had no more dedicated devotee than Jezebel and none could match her zeal for worship of Asherah. Not content with passively waiting for Israelites to convert to Baal and Asherah, Jezebel persecuted and killed Yahweh's priests.

An episode that showed Jezebel's character was the aftermath of a faceoff between hundreds of Baal and Asherah prophets versus Elijah, God's prophet, on Mount Carmel. Baal prophets were unable to influence their god to light a sacrificial fire despite trying all day. In contrast, the first time Elijah asked God to burn his sacrifice, fire from heaven consumed it. In response to seeing the glory of God, Israelites who watched the struggle, fell down and worshiped God. Immediately, Elijah ordered these Israelites to seize the prophets of Baal and Asherah and slaughter them.

Only men were on Mount Carmel, so Jezebel didn't have first-hand knowledge of what happened there. When Ahab told her about the death of her prophets, Jezebel sent a messenger to Elijah. The message was, "May the gods deal with me, be it ever so severely, if by this time tomorrow I do not make your life like one of them" (1 Kings 19:2). In essence, Jezebel threatened to kill Elijah within the next 24 hours because Elijah incited the men of Israel to kill Baal's prophets. There was nothing subtle about Jezebel's threat and Elijah believed it because past experience showed that Jezebel had the power to do what she threatened. Elijah fled from Jezebel and the Northern Kingdom, passed through Judah, and finally hid on Mount Horeb in the Sinai wasteland.

After Jezebel threatened to kill Elijah for the murder of Baal's priests, the Bible didn't record information about Jezebel for several chapters. Then, her influence was again revealed. King Ahab and Queen Jezebel were at their palace in Jezreel. There, King Ahab attempted to purchase a vineyard owned by Naboth of Jezreel. The vineyard was part of Naboth's ancestral inheritance. Rather than understanding that Naboth followed Israelite law when he declined to sell the vineyard, King Ahab went to the Jezreel palace, laid on his bed, sulked, and refused to eat.

Jezebel's next action suggested that she genuinely cared about Ahab. Jezebel went to Ahab's bedroom to learn what was wrong with him. Most wives would have done the same thing if their husband stayed in bed. They would want to know if he was sick, or how they could help him. Should they call a doctor? Jezebel asked Ahab what occurred to make him take to his bed. Ahab admitted he was piqued, or saddened, because Naboth refused to sell him a certain vineyard.

When Jezebel heard the cause of Ahab's behavior, she told Ahab to act like the king and ruler of Israel that he was, i.e., get up, cheer up, and eat. She had little patience with Ahab's behavior. Jezebel told Ahab, "I will give you the vineyard of Naboth the Jezreelite" (1 Kings 21:7). Jezebel's response to Ahab's childish behavior showed two facets of her character. First, Jezebel didn't know or didn't care about Israelite inheritance laws. From Sidon she brought the firm belief that a king could have anything and everything he wanted. Second, Jezebel was the dominant partner in Ahab-Jezebel's marriage. She was the one who "fixed" things that went wrong or were merely suboptimal for Ahab. Fixing problems for those we love isn't wrong; however, the way Jezebel went about fixing the cause of Ahab's pique showed her ruthless behavior.

Jezebel wrote a letter to the elders and nobles in Jezreel where Naboth lived. The letter was written in King Ahab's name and his seal was placed on it. In the letter Jezebel detailed that at a public feast, the elders/nobles should have two worthless scoundrels swear that they heard Naboth curse God and the king. The penalty for such a curse was stoning the culprit to death. Jezebel's plan was successful. Naboth was killed and possibly his sons were murdered as well. Because none of Naboth's heirs remained alive, the vineyard reverted to King Ahab.

There are multiple individuals who acted wrongly in this story; however, Jezebel was the initiator and influencer. Jezebel used role modeling as an influence technique. She demonstrated to King Ahab that as ruler, he didn't need to accept a negative outcome. A king could and should take action to get what he wanted. Most of us think that being a role model is good; yet, Jezebel showed how individuals can be negative role models.

Although Jezebel's letter to the Jezreel elders was legitimate—Ahab signed and sealed it—the letter was intimidating. In the atmosphere created by Ahab and Jezebel's rule, ordinary citizens didn't want to get a letter from the king. Intimidation is the primary influence technique of bullies. Jezebel's behavior put her firmly in that category. The consequences of not implementing the letter's detailed plans weren't stated. By this time in the Northern Kingdom, King Ahab and Queen Jezebel didn't have to elaborate consequences for not following their directions. Recipients knew if they didn't comply, consequences were dire.

Jezebel used alliance building with the Jezreel elders/nobles to secure Naboth's vineyard for Ahab. She didn't herself go to Naboth and attempt to buy the vineyard from him. She co-opted (designated) the elders of Jezreel to get the vineyard from Naboth. Although alliance building is a type of social influence, the alliance builder need not be well-liked or respected. Jezreel elders neither liked nor respected Ahab and Jezebel.

Jezebel didn't attempt to use any of the more positive social influence techniques, i.e., socializing or consulting, to get Naboth's land. Likely, Jezebel didn't socialize with the Jezreel elders even though she and Ahab had a palace in Jezreel. Jezebel couldn't appeal to social relationships with the elders to achieve her goal because Jezebel didn't have social relationships with them. Nor did she make any effort to socialize with their wives.

Many times Bible women used consulting as an influence technique. The letter Jezebel sent to the Jezreel elders was directive rather than consulting. She didn't ask the elders questions to allow them to evolve a strategy for getting Naboth's land for the king. Perhaps the elders could have come up with a strategy that permitted Naboth to sell his land to the king, while honoring traditional Israelite inheritance laws. Instead of using consulting, Jezebel's letter outlined a series of steps that resulted in Naboth and possibly his sons being stoned to death.

Because of Jezebel's ruthless influence and action, King Ahab got more than just Naboth's vineyard. Ahab got a curse from Elijah. Elijah told King Ahab that God would bring disaster on him and wipe out Ahab's (and Jezebel's) descendants. Plus, dogs would devour Jezebel by the palace wall. King Ahab was petrified by Elijah's prophecy. He tore his clothes, put on sack clothes, and fasted. Ahab lay in sack cloth, became very meek, and repented his sinful ways. Ahab's behavior was so changed that God told Elijah that he wouldn't bring disaster on Ahab during his lifetime; however, the disaster would occur during his sons' rule. Despite Ahab's repentance and return to worship of God, Jezebel didn't repent. She continued to worship Baal and Asherah.

Eventually, Ahab was killed in battle and his eldest son Ahaziah became king. Jezebel taught both of her sons to worship Phoenician idols. Neither son (Ahaziah and Joram) repented their idol worship, nor turned to God worship. The years that their father (Ahab) spent worshiping God had no impact on his sons. Ahaziah reigned over Israel two years, and then died. During these two years, the Bible was silent about Jezebel. Perhaps, Jezebel took no actions as egregious as her indirect murder of Naboth. On the other hand, perhaps with Ahab's death Jezebel lost some of her role power. In the Northern Kingdom, the mother of a king didn't have the same power or status as the Queen Mother in Judah.

Because Ahaziah had no sons, after his death Joram succeeded him as king. Joram reigned 11-12 years. While King Joram recovered from a battle wound in Jezreel, a prophet sent from Elisha anointed Jehu, a military commander, king of Israel. The prophet who anointed Jehu told him to strike down the house of Ahab "thus will I avenge on Jezebel the blood of My servants the prophets" (2 Kings 9:6-7). God didn't forget that Jezebel searched out and slayed many of his prophets.

Shortly after Jehu was anointed king of Israel, he confronted King Joram. King Joram asked Jehu if he came in peace. Jehu's answer was, "How can there be peace as long as all the idolatry and witchcraft of your mother Jezebel abound?" (2 Kings 9:22). Then, Jehu shot an arrow through Joram's heart and ordered Joram's unburied body to be dumped in Naboth's vineyard. If Jehu's words were representative of the Israelite military, the armed forces disliked Jezebel and the entire Ahab royal family.

Jehu was correct in naming Jezebel an idolater; however, calling her a witch was problematic. In the Bible, no verses with the exception of this one accused Jezebel of witchcraft. In the Israelite nations (both Northern and Southern Kingdoms), witchcraft was an abhorrent sin. Before the Israelites entered Canaan, Moses told them to not let anyone be found among them who practices "divination or sorcery, interprets omens, engages in witchcraft, or casts spells, or who is a medium or spiritist or who consults the dead. Anyone who does these things is detestable to the Lord" (Deuteronomy 18:9-12). The penalty for practicing witchcraft under the Mosaic Law was death (Exodus 22:18; Leviticus 20:27). By calling Jezebel a witch, perhaps Jehu justified his future murder of her.

In various Bible translations, Jezebel is called a whore; however, this label was more symbolic than reality. God's prophets used sexual metaphors and descriptions to explain Israelites' worship of idols and foreign gods. Certainly, Jezebel was one of the chief, if not the chief proponent, of idolatry in the Northern Kingdom. Despite the vitriol against Jezebel by Bible writers, accusing her of extramarital affairs wasn't justified. The Bible contained no evidence that Jezebel was disloyal sexually to Ahab during his life or even after his death. In fact quite the opposite, Jezebel was a loyal and helpful spouse, though her brand of assistance was deplorable, i.e., securing Naboth's vineyard for Ahab.

After Jehu killed King Joram, Jezebel was alone. Her husband was dead; her sons were dead. She was a former queen who treated her subjects abysmally. Jezebel knew that Jehu was coming to kill her. She determined to die as a queen. She would neither cringed nor flee. Jezebel put on eye makeup and arranged her hair. Then, she sat at a palace window and waited for Jehu to arrive in his chariot. Jezebel had no expectation that anyone would defend her or aid her escape back to Phoenician-held territory.

When Jehu entered the palace gate at Jezreel, Jezebel asked, "Have you come in peace, you Zimri, you murderer of your master?" (2 Kings 9:30-33). To the end of her life, Jezebel was decisive, aggressive, and in no way a victim. Calling Jehu "Zimri" was an insult. The insult reminded Jehu that Zimri's reign lasted only seven days before he was murdered by the military. Jezebel words implied that Jehu's reign would be as short-lived as Zimri's.

Unlike his response to King Joram who asked if Jehu came in peace, Jehu didn't bother answering Jezebel. Instead he called out, "Who is on my side? Who?" (2 Kings 9:32). When two or three of Jezebel's attendants looked out the window, Jehu ordered them to throw Jezebel to the ground. The window where Jezebel sat must have been high off of the ground and/or Jezebel's attendants really did throw rather than push her from the window. The Bible recorded that some of Jezebel's blood spattered on the palace wall. As Jezebel lay on the stones of the palace courtyard, horses trampled her dead or dying body. Later, dogs ate most of her body so that only Jezebels hands, feet, and skull were left to bury.

Conclusion

Jezebel had vision, she was decisive, and she took action. Combining these attribute, we can conclude that Jezebel had tremendous will power. When readers in the 21st century hear or read Jezebel's name, they respond by thinking of unrestrained power and an evil, decadent person. Those visceral responses are accurate, but don't include all of Jezebel's characteristics. She was rational and very consistent in her behavior. Although Ahab went back and forth in his belief in the God of Israel, Jezebel never wavered in her allegiance to Baal and Asherah. Jezebel was dedicated to the Phoenician gods and made no effort to accommodate herself to the God of Israel. From her perspective, exporting worship of her gods to the more provincial Israelite lands was something that she should do.

Mostly, Jezebel was hated and feared by ordinary Israel citizens. The hate was justified by Jezebel's actions. She believed royalty like herself could and should have anything that they wanted. Jezebel used both positive and negative influence techniques, carefully applying the technique that furthered her goals. Nowhere in Jezreel or in the Northern Kingdom is there a burial site for this once-powerful queen. King Jehu decreed that Jezebel's body should be like refuse on the ground in Jezreel. She shouldn't have a burial site or crypt that individuals should point to and say, "This is Jezebel (2 Kings 9:37).

Chapter 12

Esther, From Influenced to Influencer

The book of Esther

The book of Esther is about a beautiful Jewish girl who became the
wife of Xerxes (Ahasuerus), King of Persia (486-465 BC). Esther
saved the lives of the Jewish people in the Persian Empire and
initiated the Festival of Purim, which has been celebrated for 2500
years. She had power and influence, but she didn't start out with
either.

The story of Esther began with King Xerxes giving an elaborate
banquet for his nobles and officials. The banquet was held in the
palace's enclosed garden. His queen, Vashti, gave a banquet for the
women in another part of the palace. Feeling merry from wine,
Ahasuerus commanded that Vashti come before his banquet to
display her beauty. Vashti refused. Because of her disobedience,
Xerxes divorced Vashti. Subsequently, Xerxes went to war with the
Greeks. When Xerxes came back to Susa after an unsuccessful
campaign against the Greeks, he was lonely.

With the king's approval, his attendants initiated a search to bring
the most beautiful virgins in the Persian Empire to Susa. After 12
months of beauty treatments and learning the proper way to conduct
themselves in a royal court, a girl would spend a night with King
Xerxes. From this group of lovely virgins, King Xerxes planned to
select his next queen.

Mordecai was a Jew who lived in Susa. Possibly he was a civil
servant for the Empire. Nebuchadnezzar took Mordecai into
Babylonian captivity at the same time as King Jehoiachin of Judah.
When Esther's parents died, Mordecai reared Esther. Mordecai and
Esther were cousins, but Mordecai treated Esther as a daughter. The
Bible described Esther as lovely in form and features. When Esther
was taken from Mordecai's home into the Susa palace, Mordecai
directed Esther to tell no one that she was a Jew. Esther obeyed him.

Because Esther lived in Susa, her 12 months of beauty treatment began and ended earlier than virgins that lived in the distant provinces of the Empire. Esther won the favor of Hegai, eunuch over the harem. He treated her differently than other virgins in four ways. First, Hegai started Esther's year of beauty treatments immediately; thus expediting her introduction to King Xerxes. Second, Hegai gave Esther special food. Third, he assigned her seven maids. Fourth, Hegai moved Esther and her maids into the best suite of rooms in the harem.

During her year-long preparation, the Bible recorded that Esther won the favor of everyone who saw her. What did this teen-ager do? How did she act that caused the author of Esther to conclude that everyone in the palace viewed her favorably? True, Esther was beautiful, but so were all the girls in the harem—this was a beauty contest where the criterion for admission was physical beauty. Esther did something to set her apart from the other beautiful virgins. Some possible answers include:

First, Esther exhibited the norms of Susa, Persia. It is doubtful that she adhered to any of her Jewish roots. She didn't keep the week-long festival of Passover or hold to the Jewish Sabbath which began on the sixth day of the week at dusk and continued to dusk on the seventh day. Probably, if shell fish or pork were served at meals, she ate them. Esther asked for nothing peculiar to a home province where she originated. Esther's customs were those of Hegai and of the city of Susa. Esther fit in.

Second, Esther didn't cry from homesickness as some girls may have. The Bible gives no indication that she resented being in a virgin harem and her possible fate of going to a concubine harem if King Xerxes didn't select her as queen. She wasn't despondent that she may never be a wife, mother, or manage a household. She exhibited no resentment that she may have to marry a Persian, someone outside her nationality. Esther was low maintenance for Hegai.

Likely, Esther socialized with the other girls brought to the palace. She listened to their fears, helped alleviate their despondency, and reduced their demands; thus, Esther built an alliance with Hegai as he attempted to deal with these diverse young women. Esther role modeled how a young woman selected for the honor of being the king's chief wife should act.

On the night a virgin went to the king, the virgin could take with her anything she desired. Possibly some virgins took cosmetics and perfume; others may have taken beautiful night gowns and jewelry. Some may have taken the Persian equivalent of a toothbrush and mouth wash. The Bible didn't identify what Esther took with her to King Xerxes' chamber. We are told only that Esther took what Hegai recommended. Perhaps, Esther concluded that Hegai knew what appealed to King Xerxes. Esther trusted Hegai to provide her with the best advice available. The outcome of the night Esther spent with King Xerxes was that she became Queen of Persia (circa 479 BC).

In this initial narrative of Esther becoming Queen of Persia, we see a young girl who was beautiful and had an attractive personality. Her elderly cousin, Mordecai, loved her deeply and tried to protect her. In the Susa royal palace, Hegai favored her. Perhaps, Esther knew she had attraction power and capitalized on it to get special treatment. On the other hand, the Bible painted a picture of a young woman who obeyed the men in her life, first Mordecai, then Hegai. There is no evidence that Esther did anything proactive or pushed back by disagreeing with either Mordecai or Hegai's instructions. She was more influenced by others, than a source of influence.

Time went by in the Persian Empire. Although Esther was queen, King Xerxes assembled a second group of beautiful virgins from across the empire. Mordecai foiled a plot to kill King Xerxes. Haman became the king's closest advisor; he had a place of honor in the Persian kingdom second only to Xerxes. From time to time, King Xerxes gave banquets that included his wives, concubines, and nobles. Haman met Esther; possibly, he even spoke with her. Although Haman knew that Mordecai was a Jew, he didn't reason that Queen Esther was a Jew. Perhaps, Haman rose to power after Esther was made queen and her origin wasn't common knowledge in the Susa Court. Haman was unaware that Mordecai and Queen Esther were cousins.

In the 12th year of King Xerxes' reign, Haman persuaded King Xerxes to allow him to murder all Jews who lived in the Persian Empire. In response to the devastating news, Mordecai dressed in sack clothes and went through Susa wailing loudly. When he got to the King's gate he sat down outside the gate. He went no further because no one in sack clothes was permitted to enter the King's compound. By this time, Esther was in her fourth or early fifth year as Queen of Persia. Clearly, she wasn't King Xerxes' confidant, nor was she in the gossip loop in the Persian court. She didn't know about the planned murder of all Jews in the Persian Empire.

When Esther learned Mordecai was dressed in sack cloth, she sent clothes to him. Mordecai refused to accept the clothes; he remained in his sack clothes. Esther ordered Hathach to find out what was troubling Mordecai. Hathach was a eunuch in the Persian court assigned to Queen Esther. As queen, Esther had position power over Hathach; however, as we read through Esther-Hathach's interactions, he seemed more of a valued colleague than a servant. Hathach became the trusted intermediary between Mordecai and Queen Esther.

Reading about the circuitous conversation between Queen Esther and Mordecai, we in the 21st century automatically ask ourselves why Queen Esther and Mordecai didn't meet and discuss the problem and strategize solutions. Queen Esther and Mordecai parted on good terms so their relationship wasn't strained. Queen Esther could have ordered her cousin to come to her and explain why he was so disturbed. The answer is that Queen Esther adhered carefully to the values and norms of the Persian court. One norm was that the penalty for a courtier attempting to meet alone with a royal woman was death. If Esther flaunted this court custom, likely she would alienate Hathach who was a seasoned court servant. By Queen Esther communicating as she did, she built an alliance with Hathach and possibly won his support for her solution to the problem.

Probably, none of the messages between Queen Esther and Mordecai were written for two reasons. First, Queen Esther and Mordecai both feared that written messages could fall into the hands of an enemy. Second, Esther couldn't write. Through Hathach, Mordecai sent word to Queen Esther about the king's edict to kill the Jews. Mordecai showed Hathach the published edict that went out to every part of the Persian Empire. Mordecai directed Hathach to tell Queen Esther to go to King Xerxes and beg for mercy for her people.

When Hathach took Mordecai's message to Queen Esther, her first reaction was self-preservation. She could be killed if she approached King Xerxes uninvited! Esther's fears were elaborated in the return message she gave Hathach to take to Mordecai. In the message Esther didn't tell Mordecai directly that she didn't want to go into the king's audience hall and risk death. Instead, Esther used a number of influence techniques in her response to Mordecai, i.e., logical persuading, legitimizing, and stating. She reminded her cousin that court protocol allowed no one to appear before the king uninvited. If anyone did so, the person risked being killed unless the king didn't extend his golden scepter to the person and spare his/her life.

Esther had no expectation that King Xerxes would allow her to approach him. King Xerxes had not called Esther to him for thirty days. Esther thought back to Queen Vashti who King Xerxes divorced because she wouldn't appear before the king. Now, Mordecai wanted her to appear before the king uninvited. The irony of the two events wasn't lost on Esther.

Esther knew that when Vashti was deposed, Vashti was in a better position than Esther's current one. Vashti was the mother of several of Xerxes' sons. During the 4-5 years that Esther was married to Xerxes, she bore the king no sons. Further, King Xerxes didn't stop bringing the most beautiful virgins in the Persian Empire to the palace when he made Esther his queen.

Hathach delivered Esther's message to Mordecai. Rather than backing away from urging Queen Esther to go to the King, Mordecai continued his attempt to influence Esther to appeal directly to King Xerxes to save the Jews. After several messages back and forth between Esther and Mordecai, Queen Esther agreed to approach King Xerxes. It's difficult to know which one of Mordecai's arguments caused Queen Esther to risk her life. Was it that she too would be killed if all Jews were killed, or that her father's house would be destroyed in the pogrom? Perhaps, Mordecai's words that Queen Esther came to her royal position "for such a time as this" (Esther 4:14) was the deciding argument that caused Queen Esther to take action.

Esther agreed to approach King Xerxes if Susa Jews first fasted for three days. Esther and her maids would also fast. The fast would be from both food and water. More than likely when the Jew's fasted, they prayed that Mordecai's plan would work and the Jews in the Persian Empire would be spared. The prayers of the Jews and of Esther would have been to the Israelite God. When Esther required the Susa Jews to fast for three days, she used the influence technique of building alliances. In addition to herself, Jews throughout Susa asked God for Esther to find a successful strategy to save the lives of the Jews in the Empire.

After three days of fasting and prayer by Mordecai, Susa Jews, and herself, Queen Esther robed herself in her best finery and went to the king court. King Xerxes was seated on his royal throne. When he saw Queen Esther, he was pleased and held out his golden scepter, indicating Esther could approach him. Xerxes asked Esther her request. He assured Esther that he would give her anything she asked even up to one half of his kingdom. Giving Esther anything she asked for up to half his kingdom was a common overstatement that meant that he would give Esther whatever she desired. In all probability King Xerxes thought that Esther wanted to use her influence or intercede with him to benefit one of her court favorites. Esther responded by inviting King Xerxes and his chief advisor, Haman, to a banquet she prepared for them that day.

Why didn't Esther ask King Xerxes to lift the death sentence from the Jews in the Empire when she first entered the king's court? Why the charade of hosting him at a banquet? The answer could be that Esther wanted to pique King Xerxes' curiosity. A king who could have anything he desired had little to ponder. Not knowing what Esther wanted gave King Xerxes something to think about and kept his mind focused on his queen. Also, possibly Esther wanted to get some impression on how Xerxes felt about her. Was the king still interested in her as a woman? Had he moved on from her being his favorite to another girl/woman? When King Xerxes learned that his edict to kill Jews included killing his Queen, would Xerxes see it as a way of getting rid of Esther so he could select another queen?

At the first banquet that Queen Esther gave for King Xerxes and Haman, King Xerxes pressed the Queen to tell him her request. Again she demurred, but promised that if he and Haman would come to another banquet the next day, she would tell him her petition. Perhaps, Esther needed assurance that King Xerxes had enough interest in her to spend two days in a row in her company. Perhaps like me, Esther may have wondered if Xerxes would spend part of the night with Esther after her banquet for him. The Bible didn't record if Xerxes stayed with Esther after the banquet. The Bible recorded only that king Xerxes couldn't sleep that night. To cope with his restlessness, King Xerxes ordered a book chronicling his reign read to him.

At the second banquet that Esther gave for King Xerxes and Haman, Esther told King Xerxes about the plan to kill all Jews which included herself. She asked King Xerxes to spare her life and the lives of her people. When Xerxes asked what man would dare to make an attempt on the Queen's life and the life of her people, Esther answered that Haman did this. King Xerxes was furious and walked into the garden to compose himself.

Rather than going with King Xerxes, Haman remained inside the room with Esther, flaunting Persian rules for court behavior that no man except the king be in the same room as a royal woman. Haman fell on Esther's banquet couch to beg her to save his life just as King Xerxes re-entered the room. Xerxes accused Haman of molesting the Queen and had him hung. King Xerxes gave Haman's estate to Queen Esther.

Esther used both attraction and role power to entice King Xerxes to both banquets. During her three days of fasting and prayer, I believe Queen Esther "grew up" so to speak. She realized life wasn't all about her and she had the power to save her people. Perhaps, Esther pondered Mordecai's words that she was queen "for such a time as this" (Esther 4:14). During these three-to-five days in Esther's life, she moved from a self-focused and possibly naïve girl who followed the instructions of men in her life to being the Queen of the mightiest Empire in the known world. Despite Esther's decision to start thinking of others, King Xerxes' clear choice of her over Haman had to reinforce Esther's thoughts and actions.

Esther's actions after the second banquet demonstrated her new maturity and determination to protect Jews in the Persian Empire. On her knees, she pleaded with King Xerxes to put an end to

Haman's plan to have all Jews murdered. In response King Xerxes wrote another edict which allowed Jews throughout the Empire to kill any armed forces that might attack them. In the city of Susa alone, the Jews killed 500 men, including Haman's ten sons. Yet, this reinvented Queen wasn't finished protecting her people. The day after the Jews struck down their enemies, Esther again entered King Xerxes' throne room. Again, King Xerxes vowed to give her whatever she wanted. Esther asked that the Jews in Susa be allowed an additional day to kill their enemies and to hang Haman's ten sons where all could see them. The king concurred.

After all of these events, Mordecai was placed in a position second only to King Xerxes in the Persian Kingdom. Very probably Esther was influential in Mordecai getting this position as chief counselor to Xerxes. With Esther's agreement, Mordecai wrote a letter to Jews across the Persian Empire to direct them to celebrate annually the 14th and 15th days of Adair in remembrance of how the Jews got relief from their enemies. The name of the celebration was Purim which means "lot," the way Haman determined the date for when the Jews would be killed.

Conclusion

The book of Esther depicted a young girl who matured into an insightful, confident woman. Esther transformed from a girl who was influenced by the men in her life to a queen who used her personal and positional power to influence men in her life and to save the lives of her people. She became a woman who used her will power. She both desired to save the Jews and acted to save them, even though her actions put her own life in jeopardy.

When Esther used influence techniques, in most cases they were positive ones. She used rational influence techniques in her discussions with Mordecai. With King Xerxes she used social influence techniques, such as appealing to their relationship, i.e., "if he regards me with favor," if he is pleased with me" (Esther 8:5). Queen Esther used one negative influence technique—she manipulated, or attempted to manipulate, King Xerxes with her tears so that he would write an edict to allow the Jews to protect themselves. Whatever influence tactics Queen Esther used, they worked. The lives of Jews in the Persian Empire were spared.

Three days from the writing of this chapter on Esther is the 2017 date for the celebration of Purim. Jews have been celebrating this festival for about 2500 years all because one woman realized her power and influence on a king and on an Empire.

Chapter 13

Mary, Doubtful Influencer

Luke 1:1-56, 2; Mark 3:31-32;

John 2:1-11, 19:25-27; Acts 1:14

"Mom, I'm pregnant." Mary said to her mother.
Astonished, Mary's mother responded, "Mary, you know that you
and Joseph shouldn't have had sex until the betrothal period was
over and you were married. What were you thinking?"
"Mom," Mary replied, "The baby isn't Joseph's."
Mary's mother looked at her daughter, trying to process what
possibly could have happened. "Oh, Mary, were you raped by one of
those awful Roman soldiers?"
"No, Mom. I never had sex with anyone. The father is God." Mary
replied.

Can you imagine a conversation such as this one in a small house in
Nazareth? Yet, it could have been the conversation between Mary
and her Mother. During it, Mary tried to influence her Mother to
believe she was carrying a baby who God fathered. Repeatedly,
Mary stated with conviction what she believed was fact. She
wouldn't be swayed. Mary claimed that she was visited by an angel
and agreed to the angel's proposal that she be the mother of a baby
whose father was supernatural. Mary legitimized her assertion with
Isaiah's Old Testament prophecy that a virgin would conceive the
Messiah. Mary's mother had a relationship (history power) of 13-15
years with her daughter. In those years, Mary's mother found that
her daughter's character was outstanding; yet, how could she believe
such an implausible story?

We don't know if Mary ever convinced her mother that her
pregnancy was from the Spirit of God; however, Mary's father was
told of Mary's pregnancy. He took the news to Joseph, Mary's
betrothed. Joseph denied that he was the father of Mary's child.
Mary's father told Joseph exactly what Mary told her mother.
Probably, neither man believed Mary's statement that the Spirit of

God got her pregnant. Joseph determined to set Mary aside quietly so that she wouldn't be stoned for adultery.

The order of the two subsequent events isn't clear; however, both occurred:

- Joseph had a dream in which an angel told him to marry Mary. When Joseph woke, he took Mary home to be his wife; but had no sexual intercourse with her until after Mary's son was born (Matthew 1:20-25).
- Mary left Nazareth and traveled into the region of Hebron to visit her relative Elizabeth. This trip would have likely taken four-to-five days. Probably, Mary traveled with family or acquaintances rather than make the trip alone.

If I were unfolding these scenarios, I would have Joseph marrying Mary before she visited Elizabeth. Joseph may have been happy to have his bride leave his home for two reasons. First, if Mary was gone from his house, Joseph wouldn't be tempted to have sex with his bride. Second, perhaps Joseph thought "out of sight, out of mind." Some of the incessant gossip about Mary and by extension about Joseph would cease if Mary was absent from Nazareth.

When Mary tried to influence Joseph to believe that God fathered her child, she would have used the Jewish belief that the Messiah would be born to a virgin (legitimizing) which Mary claimed to be. Joseph was of the lineage of David, even though he was a lowly carpenter and very poor. Consciously or unconsciously, Mary appealed to Joseph's belief in the prophecy that the coming Messiah would be born to King David's offspring. Joseph was a righteous man. He wanted to believe his betrothed was telling the truth, but, could he trust her? Mary could have used tears (manipulation) to convince Joseph of her innocence.

When Mary went to visit her relative Elizabeth, she escaped all the gossip and ridicule of individuals, particularly women, in Nazareth. Woman and girls who were once her friends started to shun Mary. No one wanted to be friends with a "fallen" woman. When Mary walked by them, former friends pulled their dresses out of the way so Mary wouldn't contaminate them.

In the hill country of Judah, Elizabeth was also pregnant and she was eager to see her younger relative. Elizabeth's unborn baby jumped in Elizabeth's womb when Mary, carrying the infant Messiah, entered Elizabeth's home. In Mary's response to Elizabeth's greeting, we learn of Mary's expressive power and her eloquence in statements that have come to be known as *The Magnificat* (Luke 1:46-48). Careful reading of *The Magnificat* showed that Mary attempted again to influence listeners that her child was from God. "From now on all generations will call me blessed, for the Mighty One has done great things for me" (Luke 1:48-49). Despite Mary total acceptance of God's plan, in these words we hear the hurt of a young 13-15 year-old girl.

The next several events in Mary's life were affirming to her. Joseph took her (his wife) with him to Bethlehem. Shepherds told a story of a heavenly host announcing the birth of the infant to them. In the temple both Simeon and Anna identified baby Jesus as the Messiah. Important astronomers came to Bethlehem to worship the young child. These wise men brought gifts, gold, frankincense, and myrrh, for the child. The Bible noted several places that Mary remembered these events and pondered them in her heart. Ponder means to contemplate, deliberate, or think over. Being a teen-ager, I bet Mary also concluded: "Good! I have been justified. Now, Joseph won't think that I betrayed him."

When God told Joseph to take Mary and hers son to Egypt and live there for a time, Mary didn't attempt to influence Joseph otherwise. She accepted that God appeared to Joseph and ordered the move. By God's design, the poor family had resources (gold, frankincense, and myrrh) to fund their trip to Egypt. Several years later, Joseph's family left Egypt, but rather than return to Judea, they traveled north and resettled in Nazareth. Resettling in Nazareth was hard for Mary. All of the town's women knew that she became pregnant before marriage. Her reputation as a virtuous woman was profoundly compromised in the Nazareth region.

Anything Mary said to influence others that her pregnancy was a supernatural event or that her son was the promised Messiah was met with an eye roll and the equivalent of "Yeah, right." Eventually, Mary quit trying to explain herself. By this time, Mary and Joseph had additional children. Mary could no longer think only of herself and Jesus. Claiming an immaculate conception was just too unbelievable for the townspeople of Nazareth. If Mary continued to deny that Joseph was the father of Jesus, she would keep her sin before the family and village. Mary and Joseph's other children could be harmed by her insistence that Joseph wasn't the father of Jesus. Mary's stubborn assertion could compromise her daughters' abilities to make good marriages. Mary needed to live the life God gave her as the wife of Joseph in a small village.

Joseph was devout and yearly took his family to the Jewish festival of Passover in Jerusalem. When Jesus was 12 years old, he didn't leave Jerusalem at the end of the festival with the crowd of relatives who start back to Nazareth. Initially, Mary wasn't too worried that she didn't see her son. She thought he was somewhere in the mob of family and friends. A day later, she realized Jesus was missing. Immediately, Mary and Joseph returned to Jerusalem. They looked for Jesus all over the city. Three days later, they went to the temple and saw Jesus sitting in the temple court among the teachers discussing theology with them.

Although Mary and Joseph were together, Mary reprimanded Jesus. Her exact words were, "Son, why have you treated us like this? Your father and I have been anxiously searching for you" (Luke 2:48). Mary's comment let Jesus know that he caused his parents anxiety and Jesus behavior was unacceptable. I don't think that Mary was trying to make Jesus feel guilty or manipulate him; but, she asserted that Jesus owed them parental respect. Jesus response was, "Why were you searching for me? Didn't you know I had to be in my Father's house?" (Luke 2:49). Perhaps, Jesus didn't accept that his absence caused Mary and Joseph anxiety. On the other hand, Jesus went back to Nazareth and was obedient to his parents, suggesting Mary influenced Jesus to comply with expectations for a parent-child relationship.

For the next 18 years, the Bible is silent on Mary's life. Then, we see her at a wedding in Cana of Galilee. Joseph wasn't with Mary, likely he died sometime in the preceding years. Jesus was at the wedding. On the third day of the wedding festival, the host ran out of wine. Mary approached Jesus and told him the problem. Jesus asked Mary why she was trying to involve him; it wasn't yet time for him to start his miracles. Mary didn't answer Jesus directly; but, she instructed the servants to do whatever Jesus told them to do.

In this vignette we see several important facts: (a) Mary had some sort of power in the groom's home that influenced the servants to obey her; (b) Mary built alliances with the servants to solve the problem of no wine, and (c) in spite of Mary giving no directions to Jesus, she influenced him to convert water into wine. Mary used the power of her relationship (history) with Jesus and the power of local values. Running out of wine at a Galilean wedding would have been shocking to both the groom and attendees. Jesus intervened—he converted water into wine—at this wedding because Mary influenced him to do so.

Jesus began his public ministry at about thirty years-of-age. Before that he lived in Mary's home with her and his brothers and sisters. One day after starting his public ministry, Jesus was sitting inside a house. He was told that his mother and brothers were outside and wanted to see him (Luke 8:19-21). Jesus responded that those who believed were his mother and brothers. Jesus said that a prophet was without honor among his relatives and home (Mark 6:1-4). As far as we know, Jesus didn't go outside the house to talk with his mother.

Jesus' seemingly callous words and actions toward Mary strongly suggested that Mary ceased to believe Jesus was the Son of God. How could Mary stop believing that Jesus was the Messiah? Perhaps the reason was tied to Mary's attempt to rebuild her reputation. Individuals can only rebuild a reputation if they admitted they were wrong and changed their behavior.[1] Did Mary say that she was wrong, that she lied, that God didn't come upon her and cause her pregnancy with Jesus? Did she reject Jesus as the son of God and claim him as Joseph's son? By this time Jesus was over thirty years-of-age. Joseph was dead. No living person in Nazareth was likely to dispute that Jesus was Joseph's son.

Later, Mary followed and supported Jesus in his ministry in Galilee, Perea, and Judea. Mary was among the women at the crucifixion. From the cross, Jesus addressed her as "Dear Woman" and commended her into the care of John, the apostle (John 19:25-27). From that time onward, John rather than Mary's sons, took Mary into his home and cared for her. Jesus assigning John to care for

Mary may have been because both Mary and John believed that Jesus was God's son. His brothers and sisters didn't yet believe Jesus was the Messiah.

Mary didn't go to the tomb on Sunday (Easter) morning to anoint Jesus' body. Mary knew that Jesus wasn't really dead. Her son, the son of God, wasn't in that physical dead body, so there wasn't any need to anoint the body. The Bible provided no record of Mary meeting with Jesus after his resurrection; however, can you imagine Jesus not appearing to this woman who carried him in her womb and reared him? I am convinced that Jesus sought out Mary and assured her of his continued love. Perhaps, Jesus told Mary that the Holy Spirit would again come upon her; and, this time the Spirit would never leave.

After Jesus ascended into heaven, Mary, the apostles, and Jesus' brothers had central roles in the new Christian church. Mary influenced apostles, Jesus' siblings, new believers, and unbelievers by declaring Jesus' supernatural conception. Her statements were strong because she believed them totally. She couldn't be shaken from her witness. The Bible didn't record when Mary died or where she was buried. Perhaps as early as the first century, leaders of the new Church knew that establishing the site of Mary's burial would cause followers of Jesus to worship Mary. Mary shouldn't nor couldn't be worshiped.

Conclusion

Despite having fewer Bible verses allocated to her than many Old Testament women, Mary was the most powerful and influential Bible woman. A discerning look at Mary's behavior revealed that she wasn't perfect. Probably, Mary never envisioned what saying "Yes" to the angel, Gabriel, would mean. Her life would be upended. She would have moments of intense joy and deep sorrow.

Mary's power was in her role as Jesus' mother and her close relationship (history power) with Jesus during the first thirty years of his life on earth. Mary carried the Son of God for nine months in her womb. She breast fed him, changed his diaper, watched him take his first steps, and to grow from birth to age thirty-three. As Jesus' mother, Mary was able to influence Jesus, just as Jesus was able to influence Mary.

Chapter 14

Jezebel of Thyatira, Negative Power

Revelation 2:19-25

When Christ addressed the Thyatira church in Revelation, he spoke
harshly about a woman named Jezebel. Thyatira was a small city in
Asia Minor that belonged to the kingdom of Pergamum. Ephesus
was the capital city of Pergamum. Most of us heard about Thyatira
because Lydia, a dealer in purple cloth, was from there. Paul led
Lydia and her household to a saving knowledge of Jesus Christ at
Philippi (Acts 16:14-15). Thyatira wasn't a religious or political
center. The city had few temples and probably no acropolis.

Jesus' message to Thyatira was the longest of his messages to the
seven churches in Asia Minor. He began by praising their love, faith,
deeds, service, and perseverance. He noted that members were now
doing more than they did at first. In other words, they were growing
spiritually. At the same time, Christ condemned the Thyatira church.
The situation at Thyatira was similar to that at Pergamum, except
that Christ named the false teacher in Thyatira "Jezebel." Doubtless,
Jezebel wasn't her real name. Christ gave her this name because like
the Old Testament Jezebel, her power and influence led many
followers to worship false gods.

Here is what Christ said to the church at Thyatira:

> I know your deeds, your love and faith, your
> service and perseverance, and that you are now
> doing more than you did at first. Nevertheless,
> I have this against you: You tolerate that woman
> Jezebel, who calls herself a prophet. By her
> teaching she misleads my servants into sexual
> immorality and the eating of food sacrificed
> to idols. I have given her time to repent of
> her immorality, but she is unwilling. So I will cast
> her on a bed of suffering, and I will make those
> who commit adultery with her suffer intensely,
> unless they repent of her ways. I will strike her
> children dead. Then all the churches will

know that I am he who searches hearts and
minds, and I will repay each of you according
to your deeds. Now I say to the rest of you in
Thyatira, to you who do not hold to her teaching
and have not learned Satan's so-called deep
secrets, 'I will not impose any other burden on
you, except to hold on to what you have
until I come.' - Revelation 2:19-25

Revelation readers wonder just who was this woman named Jezebel?
Was she a real person or an idea? Where did she get her power and
influence? Several scholars argued that Jezebel was the wife of the
bishop of the Thyatira church. Some early manuscripts of this
passage include, "your wife, Jezebel." Others proposed that she was
a fortune-teller.

Outside the walls of Thyatira was a small temple or enclosure
dedicated to SanBethe, a woman with the gift of prophecy. At
various times and locations in ancient Near East history, schools or
centers of women prophets formed that were dedicated to SanBethe.
Often, these schools had a distinct Jewish perspective and attracted
Jews in the area. Conceivably, Jezebel wasn't a member of the
Thyatira Christian congregation. Instead she followed SanBethe and
affiliated with other women at this small temple. These self-
identified prophetesses tried to entice members of the congregation
of Christ at Thyatira to follow them.

We won't know this side of heaven where Jezebel derived her
power; however, there are clues in Christ's message to the church at
Thyatira. Christ identified that she was a teacher. Whether she was
knowledgeable, in the sense that she had more skills, abilities,
talents, and accomplishments, is difficult to estimate. Likely, Jezebel
had expressive power. She was eloquent and able to communicate
both powerfully and effectively. Because she was a long standing
member of the Thyatira community, she had relationship (history)
power with Thyatira citizens, Christians and non-Christians.

Archeological evidence verified that Thyatira had guilds of
woolworkers, linen workers, dyers, leatherworkers, tanners, potters,
slave dealers, etc. The city's industrial base meant women pursued
careers outside the home. Women as well as men were guild

members. Each guild was dedicated to a god. The problem for Christians in Thyatira was whether or not to participate in guild banquets. Banquets included eating food dedicated to a guild idol and taking part in sexual orgies. Refusal to join and participate in guild activities made it difficult for artisans to find work.

The Jerusalem Council (49-50 AD) prohibited Christians from eating food sacrificed to idols. That meant Christian guild members couldn't join public festivals and participate in guild banquets. Non-participation in guild activities brought suspicion and dislike on the new Christian church and on its members. Further, non-participation in guild activities meant a reduction in income. Fully-participating guild members only rarely referred clients to non-participating guild members.

In response to this conundrum, Thyatira church members who were also guild members embraced Jezebel's teachings. Jezebel told them they could eat food sacrificed to idols without sinning. When making this claim, Jezebel used logical persuading, a rational influence technique. Jezebel asserted that the gods, represented by idols, didn't exist. There could be no harm in eating food sacrificed to an idol at a guild banquet because the idol didn't exist. Further, when Jesus was on earth he said that what went into a person's mouth didn't defile him or her. Rather, what came out of the body made a person unclean (Mark 7:18-20). Jezebel's rational argument and citing Jesus' own words seemed to make sense. Further, the analysis allowed guild members to remain in a guild, attend guild banquets, and retain their income stream.

In his letter to the church at Thyatira, Christ said that Jezebel led followers into sexual immorality. Many times sexual immorality occurred in conjunction with the guild banquets. After drinking and eating at sumptuous guild banquets, the norm was to have sex with multiple other guild members. Church members could have left the guild hall before sexual orgies began, but most didn't. Instead, Christians who were guild members fully participated in all guild activities, that is, they ate food, drank wine, and had sex with other guild members.

Some early church's held to the duality of man (Gnosticism). They believed that mankind had both a spiritual and physical part. Anything done in the body, even the grossest sin, has no meaning because real life existed in the spirit realm. Although Christ's words against Jezebel didn't say that she adhered to Gnosticism, she may have taught that Christians were composed of these two selves. Wanton sex, done by the physical self, had no impact on the spiritual or Christian self.

Jezebel identified herself as a prophetess. Being a prophetess meant she communicated with and received messages from a part of the Trinity; but, Jezebel was a false prophetess. No member of the Trinity—God the Father, God the Son, or God the Holy Spirit—communicated with her. She lied about her communications with God. Many 21st century Christians may ask, "Why did Thyatira Christians believe her?" The answer could be related to the SanBethe temple. Town's people were accustomed to women foretelling. Jezebel's claim to be a prophet, seer, or foreteller was acceptable, even familiar, in Thyatira society.

Jezebel searched for deeper spiritual knowledge beyond what was taught by the apostles and Paul. According to Christ, Jezebel's search moved her into Satan's realm. When Jezebel promised her followers secret spiritual knowledge, her actions and promises mimicked the Gnostics. Gnostics believed they could triumph over Satan if they studied him and knew his deep secrets. Jezebel ignored or forgot that true knowledge is found in Christ (Colossians 2:2–3; Ephesians 3:18–19). When Christ is central to a Christian's beliefs, obscure or arcane knowledge and information aren't necessary or relevant.

How did Jezebel influence Christian individuals in the new Christian church to follow her? What influence techniques did she use? We already noted that Jezebel likely used logical reasoning and legitimizing when she appealed to Jesus's own words. Perhaps, she appealed to Paul's authority also. By the time Revelation was written (90-96 AD), many of Paul's letters were widely circulated to the Christian churches. Jezebel may have quoted Paul's first letter to the Corinthians (written 45-55 AD) in which he wrote "God has revealed it to us by the Spirit. The Spirit searches all things, even the deep things of God" (1 Corinthian 2:10).

Jezebel made the argument that searching for deeper meaning was good. She legitimized her argument with Paul's own words which she took out of context. Searching had to be the right thing to do if Paul attested that the Spirit revealed things, even the deep things of God.

Jezebel used stating, another rational influence technique. She asserted what she believed and wanted in a compelling tone and with self-confidence. Stating was a rational influence technique that Jezebel of Thyatira excelled at.

Christ named this woman in the Thyatira church, Jezebel, because she had many traits of her Old Testament name sake. Like Jezebel, the wife of King Ahab in the Northern Kingdom of Israel, Jezebel of Thyatira had will power, or the determination to be powerful. Plus, she took steps or actions to cause others to follow her lead. In the Old Testament countless individuals replaced worship of the true God of Israel with worship of Baal and Asherah. In the New Testament, Jezebel's followers replaced worship of Christ with worship of both Christ and idols, a form of syncretism in which Christianity was blended with the Greek pantheon of Gods. Such worship wasn't from Christ, but from Satan.

A powerful influence technique derived from social relationships was building alliances. Jezebel of Thyatira could have built alliances with women fortunetellers in the SanBethe temple. Jezebel colluded with temple fortune tellers to say or predict many of the same things that she preached or advised. All churches have strong and weak members. Some weaker church members may have continued to seek out the foretellers at SanBethe's temple even after coming to belief in Christ. If these weak members heard the same message from temple foreseers and Jezebel, they may have concluded that if a Christian prophetess and a pagan fortune teller said the same thing, it had to be true. They were unaware that SanBethe fortunetellers and Jezebel colluded to give the same message and that the message was a lie.

Ever gracious, Christ gave "Jezebel time to repent of her immorality, but she was unwilling to do so" (Revelations 2:21). Christ said that Jezebel's sins didn't just start recently. They were long standing, during which Jezebel had time to repent. To repent or want to repent, individuals must believe that they did, or are doing, something wrong. When I pondered Jezebel of Thyatira's actions, I tend to think that she didn't believe or conceive that any of her actions were wrong. Whatever Jezebel believed about herself, Christ asserted that Jezebel was unwilling to repent. Jezebel didn't want to change her behavior.

In Revelation Jezebel's decision to disobey God brings us full circle to Eve in Genesis. Eve didn't want to obey God. Eve wanted something more, that is, fruit from the Tree of Knowledge of Good and Evil, than God said she needed or could have. Both Eve and Jezebel were willful. They wanted God, but wanted him their way, rather than God's way.

Because Jezebel wouldn't repent, her outcome was dire. Christ planned to (a) cast Jezebel on a bed of suffering; (b) make individuals who commit adultery with Jezebel suffer intensely, unless they repented of their ways; and (c) strike Jezebel's children dead. Casting Jezebel on a bed of suffering could mean she would become acutely ill, so sick she had to stay in bed. Alternatively, Jezebel's bed or suffering may have meant that she agonized when she saw followers suffer physically, mentally, and spiritually.

When Christ said that he would strike Jezebel's children dead, most likely he referred not to Jezebel's biological children, but to individuals who followed Jezebel's teachings, i.e., engaged in sexual immorality, ate food sacrificed to idols, and delved into the spiritual realm of Satan. Striking the children dead was a terrible fate, particularly if Jezebel's followers died un-repentant and mired in Satanism. While he walked the earth, Jesus said that if individuals didn't believe that he was the son of God, they would die in their sins (John 8:24). Individuals in the Thyatira church who believed that they needed something, or someone, more than Christ, the son of God, to be saved could die in their sins.

Have you ever noticed that humans love secrets? They like, really like, to feel superior to others because they know something few other people know. That is what Jezebel offered—secrets that led to added knowledge of spiritual beings and behaviors. Thus, Jezebel's followers felt superior to less enlightened members of the church. In contrast to Jezebel's position, Christ said that she and followers weren't superior. Instead, Jezebel was a liar when she averred that individuals needed "more" than belief in Christ's birth, life, death, and resurrection to get to heaven

Appealing to values is an emotional influence technique frequently used by spiritual leaders. In the late first century, Thyatira was part of the Roman Empire; yet, the region and city were strongly influenced by Greek thinking styles and techniques. Paul said Greeks look for wisdom (1 Corinthians 1:22). Jezebel of Thyatira looked for wisdom. She appealed to the desire of her Greek-thinking followers to live a Christian life through wisdom. She seemed not to understand, or perhaps she just refused to accept, that Christ's message was so simple a child could understand it. Christianity was about Christ crucified, which as Paul wrote was foolishness to Greeks (1 Corinthians 1:22-23).

Conclusion

Jesus knew the value of prophets. When he walked the earth as a man, Jesus spoke often of prophets. At the same time, Jesus cautioned people to reject false prophets. False prophets could be identified by what they produced. Jezebel of Thyatira was a false prophetess. She produced false teachings. She taught that members of the Christian church at Thyatira didn't have to follow the teachings of the Church fathers on eating food sacrificed to idols or sexual promiscuity. In Jezebel's perspective salvation required more than belief that Christ, the son of God, was crucified for the sins of the world. Real salvation required knowing deeper secrets inspired by Satan.

Pondering Jesus' words to the Thyatira church, we aren't sure if Jezebel actually participated in guild banquets or she only condoned the activity in her followers. But that difference isn't important. Jesus made no distinction between prophets who condoned idolatry and immorality and those who practiced them. When individuals want to do something, enjoy doing it, and, the activity impacts their income, little influence is required to have them fully embrace the activity. That seems to be what was happening in the Thyatira church. Church members who wanted to step away from basic Christian beliefs had a champion in Jezebel.

Conclusions

Immediately before Jesus was taken up into heaven, he told his disciples that "you will receive power when the Holy Spirit comes on you" (Acts1:8). Christ was speaking to both men and women. Both in the Christian church of the first century and the twenty-first century, women were and are given power when they receive the Holy Spirit into their lives. The Spirit is the same for men and women and the same spirit that women received millennia ago. Although this book, *Out of the Shadows*, reviewed power sources in women, there is no greater power source than the Holy Spirit. With power from the Spirit of God, women can influence the world for Christ.

When I pondered the power and influence of Bible woman, my first realization was that some of the Bible women were so very young. Esther was around 15 years-old when she became Queen of Persia. Mary, the mother of Jesus, was probably younger than 15 years-of-age when an angel asked her to be the mother of the Messiah. From my perspective of a middle aged woman, I asked myself, "How could God put these young women in this position?" Their brains weren't fully developed. Neither were their thought processes, consequently, their beliefs and behaviors weren't mature. Did they really know what they were doing or agreed to do?

I don't know the answer to my questions; but, I do know that God's thoughts are far above mine (Isaiah 55:8). My role is to trust God without having all the answers. Last Saturday I attended a teaching conference at church. The teaching leader said that maturing Christians were constantly in tension between asking God legitimate questions—even having legitimate doubts—and having our thoughts informed by what scripture tells us.[12] I need to strive for a scriptural perspective as I question and receive answers from God on the power and influence of Bible women.

Many Old and New Testament women weren't included in this book. The book isn't an exhaustive list of Bible women. There was no discussion of the Queen of Sheba, the Midianite princess Cozbi, King David's daughter Tamar, and Jacob's daughter Dinah to name only a few Old Testament omissions. While in the New Testament, the power and influence of the widow of Nain, the woman caught in adultery, and Jairus' daughter weren't described. Excluding these Bible women and many others from a book on power and influence, doesn't mean that they were without power or influence. The included women were models of women with power and influence in their environments. The women in *Out of the Shadows* provide Christian women with models to use when searching Holy Scriptures to expose the power and influence of Bible women.

References Cited

1. Bacon, Terry R. 2011. *The Elements of Power, Lessons on Leadership and Influence*. Atlanta, GA: American Management Association.

2. Roth, Carolyn A. 2015. *Lesser Known Bible Characters, Using their Relationships to Restore Ours*. Mustang, OK: Tate Publishing and Enterprises, LLC.

3. Lockyer, Herbert. 1967. *All the Women of the Bible*. Grand Rapids, MI: Zondervan.

4. McNair, Rod. 2012. Willpower. *Tomorrow's World*. Accessed on January 6, 2017. Retrieved from: http://www.tomorrowsworld.org/magazines/2012/january-february/willpower/.

5. Bacon, Terry R. 2012. *Elements of Influence, The Art of Getting Others to Follow Your Lead*. Atlanta, GA: American Management Association.

6. Strong, James. 2010. *The New Strong's Exhaustive Concordance of the Bible*. Nashville, TN: Thomas Nelson.

7. Ginzberg, Louis. n.d. *Legends of the Bible*. Single volume version published by Barnes & Noble Books. Original seven volumes published by Jewish Publication Society of America 1909, 1910, 1911, 1913, 1956. Philadelphia, PA: The Jewish Publication Society.

8. Whiston, William (Translator). 1987. *The Works of Josephus, Complete and Unabridged*. Peabody, MA: Hendrickson, Publishers, Inc.

9. Hanson, David G. 2009. Moses and Hatshepsut. *Bible Archaeology*. Accessed December 17, 2016. Retrieved from: http://www.biblearchaeology.org/post/2009/02/Moses-and-Hatshepsut.aspx/.

10. Posner, Menachem. n.d. Who sent Zipporah away? Accessed March 22, 2016. Retrieved from: http://www.chabad.org/parshah/article_cdo/aid/1411628/jewish/Who-Sent-Zipporah-Away.htm/.

11. Hareuveni, Nogah and Frenkley, Helen. 1989. *Tree and Shrub in our Biblical Heritage*. Kiryat Ono, Israel: Neot Kedumim, Limited.

12. McDermott, Gerald R. 2017. Divine Signs: God's Fingerprints in all Reality. Spring Teaching Seminar. Roanoke, VA: St. John Lutheran Church.

Dr. Carolyn A. Roth

Biographical Information

Dr. Carolyn A. Roth has advanced degrees in psychology and a doctorate in organizational leadership. She spent 25 years teaching leadership and management in universities. Her last full-time position was as a distinguished professor in a major university.

Carolyn is a spiritual woman who believes in the Trinity—God the Father, God the Son, and God the Holy Spirit. She believe that the words in the Bible are the inspired, irrefutable Word of God.

Out of the Shadows was written so that readers could be assured that God created a woman to be equal to a man. Women played major roles in the Bible. They used the same power and influence techniques as used by women today and used by Bible men.

Carolyn is very eager to hear your questions and comments. For more information on Dr. Roth, visit her website: www.CarolynRothMinistry.com/